Black and Red Butterflies

By Denise Mclaughlin

Printed in the United States of America

ISBN-13: 978-0692651193
ISBN-10: 0692651195

10 9 8 7 6 5 4 3 2

Empire Publishing

www.empirebookpublishing.com

Contents

Chapter 1

Dark Stranger

January 19, 2013 12:25 AM

It took two days to finally receive the phone call that I had anxiously feared. The police officer tried to contact me on my way home from work. I must have been in a dead zone since I did not get the voicemail he left until I pulled into my driveway. My heart was racing and my mouth was severely dry. I could barely get the words out when I asked the dispatcher to connect me to the officer who left me the message. After what seemed like several minutes, I finally heard a deep voice on the other end of the phone.

"Miss McLaughlin?" the officer asked. "Do you know of anyone in Duane's family that I can speak to?"

"No." I answered. "He's not from around here. He's from Pennsylvania. All of his family lives out of state and I've never met them."

The answer of course brought on more questions. How long have I known him? Who was I to him? Did he have a roommate? I was starting to get impatient. I didn't understand why he was asking me all these questions. It also irritated me that I didn't know the answers. I thought I knew Duane pretty well. It turns out I didn't really know him at all. I didn't care though. I just wanted to know if he was alright.

"Did you go to the apartment?" I interrupted.

"Yes…" the cop hesitated.

"And did you go in?" I impatiently asked. I wanted to know more but at the same time I was scared of what he would say.

"Yes we did go in." The officer didn't want to continue but he knew he had to say something. "We did go in. And unfortunately…he has passed away…"

The words *passed away* repeated slowly in my mind as if my brain couldn't grasp the meaning. *He has passed away…..he has passed away…passed away…..*

My heart dropped to my feet the second I heard those words even though I already knew deep down Duane was gone hours before the officer told me. I thought it would be easier to deal with hearing someone else say it. I was wrong. It hurts even more, especially when it was said out loud.

"How did he die?" I asked.

"Since you're not a family member I can't give you the details." he explained. "All I can say is it was on his own accord."

I was confused. "Accord?"

The office put it in easier terms for me. "He did it himself."

"Oh my god," I whispered. "I'm gonna throw up."

"Ok well," the cop stately rapidly. "If you can think of anything else you want to tell us feel free to call. If you start having thoughts of harming yourself, please don't hesitate to call 911 or go to the nearest emergency room."

I quickly thanked him and ran into my house. I rushed to the bathroom and swallowed two Xanax. I couldn't get them in my system fast enough. I wanted to down the whole bottle but forced myself to stop. I had to get out of there. I kept screaming over and over "Duane, I'm so sorry. I'm sorry I wasn't there for you." I buried my face into the couch and sobbed. I crawled up into a ball and cried for what seemed like hours. Occasionally I would stop and repeat that I was sorry. Even though what Duane did was not my fault, I still felt responsible. He was crying out for help several times and I rushed out of his apartment instead of holding him when he needed me the most. I could have prevented what had happened but chose to turn my back on him. I called my close friend Valerie and filled her in on what happened. She repeated the information to her parents and they insisted I stay the night with them. If I had not found a friend to be with that night, I sincerely believe I would've taken my own life from the guilt that consumed me.

July 14, 2012

Six Months Earlier

The first time I met Duane, I can honestly say I didn't think too highly of him. That is completely against everything we all stood for at the housing center where I worked. As social workers, we are taught not to judge clients. Sometimes that was difficult when we would see similar situations and hear the same stories clients told us every day. Stories about how they ended up in a homeless shelter in the first place. It wasn't Duane's story that disturbed me. It was his attitude. It was very negative. It only takes seven seconds after meeting someone for the first time that we, as humans, start making judgments.

The first time I heard Duane's voice over the phone was when I made my judgment about him. I had to do an intake with him before I could get him checked into our facility. He answered all my questions but with hesitance. He made it obvious he didn't want to talk to me. Nevertheless, it was part of our program policy to get these questions answered. It was the typical questions such as name, birth date, and address. Then the questions get more personal. The form asks about any former drug abuse or medical conditions. The form even asked about sexual orientation. I never understood why that would matter but there it was. I guess I would get irritated if a stranger asked me that too. However, Duane had a bad temper and didn't need to express them with me. I didn't help the matter much. I was hung over from the night before and really didn't want to work that day. That was no excuse though. I was the professional and needed to stay calm no matter how rude Duane was with me. He made it extremely difficult for me to remain calm and positive.

When Duane arrived at the shelter, he was a lot younger than he sounded on the phone. He had an accent that is often heard in people from New York or the surrounding area. It wasn't noticeable earlier on the phone but I definitely caught it when he was sitting in front of me. When he spoke, I felt like I was watching an episode of *The Jersey Shore*. His accent was faint but it was prominent when he said specific words. It also became more apparent when he spoke faster or was getting upset or irritated. He had a gap in between his front teeth, that depending on the angle he was sitting, it almost looked like he had a tooth missing. He was about six feet tall and very thin. He had appeared to have had a rough couple of days; or even years. He had dark circles under his eyes and very pale skin. Most clients who came to us looked shaken, tired, and malnourished. So it was not alarming to see Duane this way. Some clients also looked completely the opposite from that. Some appeared very healthy, happy, and dressed in expensive clothing. Homeless has no face. It is not always the dirty bearded man sitting in the alley with a pint in his hand. Someone who is homeless can look like an everyday you or I. As for Duane, I could not see past the dreary, lonesome, and angry vibe he threw out. Even though he was smiling at me, I could see the despair in his eyes.

He gave me documents that I needed and told me his story although it had many gaps in it. I wanted to ask for more information and fill in the blanks but I knew Duane would let me know more when he was ready. Many clients are in shock when they enter a place like this so it was not unusual for his story to not make much sense. As I went through the documents he gave me and made copies for his file, I noticed he had papers from previous therapists. It concerned me because one of the intake questions I asked him earlier was if he had any medical conditions. The answer he had given me was no.

"Can you explain this paperwork to me?" I asked him. I didn't want to mention the fact that he withheld information from me since I was concerned he would get upset.

"I was diagnosed with PTSD." Duane quietly stated.

PTSD, also known as Post Traumatic Stress Disorder, is a mental illness usually associated with soldiers or those who had endured severe trauma.

"Were you in the army?" I asked.

Duane shook his head. "People always ask me that." he smirked. "No. I went through some things."

"What kind of things?" I wondered.

Duane showed me his right arm. From the wrist up to his forearm was a huge scar. I asked him what happened and he said he got stabbed a few years ago. When I asked him by whom, he just said a crazy person did it. He didn't want to go further into the story so we moved on. I felt so bad for him. How terrible to be attacked in such a way. I continued to go through the documents. I came upon a letter typed up by a psychiatrist stating that Duane was no danger to himself and others.

"What is this about?" I continued.

"I've had anger problems in the past," he answered honestly.

"Anger problems?" I repeated, confused.

"I've gotten into a lot of fights," he reluctantly replied.

This concerned me since there was a no violence policy at the shelter. I explained to Duane that being immediately exited from our program for fighting was something we were strict about. He went on to tell me all the fights he had been in were him trying to defend himself. He admitted he had a hard time walking away from someone who was provoking him. I strongly advised that if anyone here was causing him issues like that to come right into the office and let staff handle it. He nodded and assured me he would do so.

I gave Duane his bedding and personal hygiene products. We walked around the property and I showed him where things were. I then showed him to his room, which was room one. It was the largest men's room we had and it was usually full. After that day, I didn't see Duane much. When I did see him on grounds, he either looked really sad or angry. He wore inappropriate shirts and I had to ask him to change. Once he entered the office angry because other clients told him he needed to speak to his wraparound leader Rosie about finding a place to live and he didn't know who she was.

"Who the fuck is Rosie and what the fuck is a wraparound leader?" he shouted at me.

I calmly asked him to watch his language while I answered all of his questions. I told him I understood that our rules were confusing but getting upset at people who are only trying to help was not going to get him anywhere. A few days later, he came into the office one day to pick out movies and gave me a hard time about staff removing the rated R videos from our shelves.

"Can I watch Barbie?" he mocked. "Or is that rated R too?"

This was the usual Duane attitude and I was getting tired of it. I told him if he didn't like our program, he was free to exit at any time. According to daily staff notes, the other employees documented that they had issues communicating with Duane too. His roommates also had a hard time with him. He didn't want to be there or follow the rules. He didn't stay long. He was there about two weeks. He said he had to go downstate and take care of some legal issues. Nobody tried to get him to stay. We all wanted him gone. We were glad to see him go. He just seemed like many of the people who came to our shelter looking for help. They didn't really want help. They wanted a free place to stay for the maximum ninety days before moving on to the next closest shelter and repeating the process.

Chapter 2

Falling for Darkness

As much as I hoped Duane was gone for good, he came back a week later. My manager, Chad had approved it. After speaking to Duane on the phone, Chad, said that he felt that Duane was sincere about changing his life around. This was the opposite of what he had said a few days prior. He was just as relieved to see Duane go as the rest of us. I was very surprised when I saw the troubled man standing at the door waiting to be motioned in. Since I was the one on duty, I had to do the intake process all over again. My stomach was in knots about this. I did not like Duane. He scared me. He had a short fuse. The littlest things got him upset. Everyone had to watch what they said around him so he wouldn't lose his temper.

So here I was, sitting at the desk with him once again. The good news was since he already had a file that was less than a year old, I just had to initial and date any information that had changed. He took care of his legal matters and this time brought his green ford escort back with him. He had put temporary insurance on it, making the vehicle legal for a week just to get it up here and it was about to expire. Because of that, he would have to let it sit in our parking lot until it had permanent insurance. If he was seen driving it, he would have to exit or park elsewhere. This was a safety issue. Our company could be liable if he was to get into an accident in that car while entering or leaving the shelter.

Duane still had that edge to him but he seemed happier, healthier, and ready to make a change. He had also gotten haircut and looked completely different. For the first time, I noticed how attractive he was, especially when he smiled. *He should try smiling more often* I thought. He was more approachable that way. I gave him some bedding and personal items. I put him in room five that time, which was our other men's room. His previous room was full. I also thought if I put him in a new group of men, he could get a fresh start at making friendships with people who didn't already have assumptions about him.

Duane did do better a second time around at the shelter. He made it to the morning meetings and charted on time every day. Charting is when the clients tell staff what they accomplished that day in reaching their goal of leaving the shelter and becoming more self-sufficient. For example, some clients would say they job searched that day. They provided a list of contact information that staff could follow up with as proof that they did actually look for work. Some clients were on disability and didn't have to job search. However, they were required to meet with the housing specialist on finding affordable housing. All clients had to save 70% of their income, which was then returned to them on exit and the money was used for a security deposit on an apartment. Duane was on disability for PTSD, so this would be his main goal as well.

Clients also talked about their interests. They talked about their likes and dislikes. They talked about anything they felt that they wanted to say. I learned that Duane was very interested in music as was I. It turned out we both enjoyed heavy rock. Sometimes we would just sit for a few extra minutes and talk about new material artists were coming out with. We would discuss new songs we liked or didn't like and why. We also liked a lot of the same movies and thought the same things were funny. Sometimes when I would talk to him, I felt like I was looking in a mirror and talking to myself. We had a lot of the same opinions and views on a variety of different topics. After a while, I looked forward to Duane's chats. Even though he put up a wall most of the time, he wasn't a bad guy. He was actually quite interesting and sweet. I was breaking boundaries by letting him know so much about me and vice versa. Getting personal with clients is never a good thing. Even though I knew it was inappropriate I didn't want to stop talking to Duane.

I remember one session when I asked him what he did that day. He couldn't think of anything to tell me. The sarcastic side came out and he finally said, "I dunno...smoked crack I guess."

It was funny because I knew it wasn't true. To be silly, I wrote in the file *Socialized.* We both cracked up.

"Sure," he agreed laughing hysterically. "I guess that's what people are calling it now these days."

Another time I was wearing a purple blouse and purple eye shadow to match. Instead of putting my hair in the usual bun, I had some flowing around the side of my face. Duane noticed and kept asking if I was going on a date.

"You look good," he said with a smile.

It made me smile back. A little too much I think. I felt flattered and was excited that he noticed. "Thank you." I said shyly.

He held eye contact with me for a few seconds as he said smiling, 'You're welcome."

At that second, I think that was when I started having feelings for him. It may have started before that. I'm not sure. My heart skipped a beat when he appeared. Then it would race and it was difficult to focus on anything else. I would think about Duane when I was at home. I usually didn't think about work or clients. But I often thought about him. I didn't think about him in any particular way. Just his name entered my mind. Then the thoughts would progress and I would end up wondering what he was doing at that very moment. However the night he complimented me, I started thinking about him sexually. I was flattered Duane noticed me and I wanted him. I thought about him when I was having sex with my husband. I thought about him when I was pleasing myself. When I climaxed, I would say his name and command him to fuck me faster. These dirty thoughts made me climax harder and I wanted to make them a reality. These thoughts started happening at work when I would see Duane on grounds or when he walked by the office window. He always seemed to make eye contact with me. It was if he were thinking about me too. I must not have been the only one to notice this. My manager noticed it too. There was one afternoon that he and Duane came out of the office after a one on one meeting. As Duane was walking out, he saw me sitting at the desk.

"Well hello Denise," he said coolly walking over to me. He hung around for a few minutes trying to think of things to talk to me about. I tried to be polite and calm but I knew Chad was watching us and I didn't want my real feelings to show. Eventually Duane left and Chad mentioned he did not want me being Duane's wraparound leader. A wraparound leader is a staff member who works one on one with clients. Usually, as clients enter the program, each staff member takes turns helping them. Duane was supposed to be on my list. However, Chad was concerned about the way Duane looked at me and wanted to hang around me. He could tell

12

Duane had a crush. If he knew I felt the same, he was careful not to reveal it to me.

For the next few days, I watched Duane from the windows of the office and also from the window upstairs in the attic. I tried to distance myself because I was married. I knew if I could have the chance to be alone with Duane, I would take it. I did not trust myself with him. When Duane would walk past me, I ached for his touch. I felt so disappointed when he didn't. Sometimes the disappointment was so unbearable that my body felt like it was in pain from not being touched. I think Duane felt it too. He had to have liked me. When we would converse, it seemed like we spent more time staring into each other's eyes than we did actually speaking. His eyes would find mine and just *stare.* Our eyes would communicate silently as to say *I want you and I want you right now.* Then of course someone would come into the office and ruin the moment. Maybe that was a good. We both seemed to forget where we were and who we were. Since everything and everyone else around us would freeze in time when we were together, people interrupting our moment forced us back to reality.

As the next few days passed, I would find reasons to walk the grounds or enter Duane's room. I would restock the emergency kit whether it needed it or not. I would make sure smoke detectors were working even when they had already been examined. When I did room inspections, I took extra time in his room. I would purposely bend over furniture and pretend I was examining the cleanliness of everything, just hoping he was looking at my ass. I walked by the room a lot so I could be nosy and peer in as I walked by. I always smiled at Duane when I did this. On one occasion, I knew he was washing his clothes in the laundry room. I was curious if he were still in there. I was hoping he was. I wanted to make my move on him. If he happened to freak out and tell someone, I would deny it. Since it was a secluded spot, nobody could witness my inappropriate behavior. Unfortunately he was not in there. He must have been watching me though. When I came out of the laundry room, he was coming in to check his laundry. As I turned the corner to go back to the office, I looked over my shoulder and smiled seductively at him. I knew he was watching me walk away and I wanted him to know I knew he was watching.

Later that night when Duane came to chart, we went about our usual business. He mentioned that he wanted to be taken off transportation for the next day. The transportation schedule was on the wall behind him. I walked over to it and searched for his name. It was towards the bottom and it was awkward for me to bend down to cross his name off. He was watching my every move. I could feel his eyes burn into my back. I decided to give him something to look at. Teasingly, I got on my knees and I crossed his name off. I wanted him to visualize what I looked like in that position. I sat back down at my desk as if I was unaware of my sexual intentions. Duane watched my every move. As we continued the charting process I could not help smiling and staring as did he.

Come on Denise, I thought to myself, *Say something. Don't sit there like an idiot.*

"I'm glad you came back," I admitted.

Duane seemed to like that. I could tell he was not used to positive feedback in his life. From what I had learned about him, he spent most of his life in negative situations such as drug use, child abuse and getting kicked out of places for losing his temper.

"You seem a lot better now." I went on. "You seemed really pissed off last time."

Duane laughed. "That's because I was pissed off."

We stared at each other some more. I wanted to wrap my arms around him and kiss him violently and let him have his way with me right there on the desk. I could tell by the way he was looking at me that he wouldn't object to that.

"You have a nice smile." I continued shyly. "You should smile more often. It looks good on you."

He didn't say anything. He continued to stare at me, his eyes burning into mine with wild intensity. I could tell he wanted to say or do something but I think he was shocked at what was going on.

"Do I make you nervous?" I asked without thinking. Oh my god, what kind of question was that?

"No." he smirked. "Why would you make me nervous?"

I looked intensely into his eyes. "Because I'm staring at you."

Duane laughed some more. "Why are you staring at me?"

I didn't know what to say. Either I had to keep quiet and withhold my true feelings or I had to come clean with my desires. I had to say something. I got his attention. I might as well tell him how I felt. He knew I was married but I know he wouldn't care. At this point, neither did I. My husband didn't exist to me right now. All I wanted was Duane. The consequences of my actions did not matter as long as I could have Duane. I wanted him inside me so bad.

"You make me want to do bad things." I whispered, looking him straight in the eyes. Then I started to giggle. He could tell I was embarrassed by what I just said. He looked surprised at my response and yet intrigued. Just then, the doorbell rang, meaning someone needed to come in. I

15

wished we were alone but I was also glad they were there. I was in over my head and needed to get out of this awkward situation. I got up from the desk and told Duane he was all set and to let the next person in. I looked at him as to say I was sorry for my behavior. I knew he could tell what I was thinking because all he said so calmly to me was, "Relax."

Right then I knew he wouldn't tell a soul about it.

Chapter 3

Weak and Powerless

I felt better letting Duane know how I felt about him yet it was difficult to concentrate for the rest of my shift. The clients saw me glowing and kept commenting on what a great mood I was in. I felt like I was in high school again and beaming over my latest crush. I wanted Duane and I wanted him tonight. I was willing to get a hotel and take him there after work. However, my plan was ruined when my husband Dave texted me to say he was on his way back from his trip. He went for a weekend camping trip downstate with a few friends. He was supposed to be gone for another night. He said he was tired and ready to come home. Dammit, I thought. This would have been perfect.

Cheating is never right; especially when I was about to do it to someone who treated me like a queen. My husband and I had been fighting a long time about the same stuff and it was only driving us further apart. I did not get along with his family or his son and it often caused tension in the home. The worst part was it put Dave in the middle. I could go on about who did what to who but there is no excuse. We were not happy and I was obviously seeking affection from someone else. What I didn't understand was why I wanted someone who had a history of mental illness and anger. Why would I want someone who had to move around a lot because there was always conflict between him and his landlords? Why want someone who didn't work and couldn't hold a job because of his illness?

My husband was the kindest and most giving person I had ever met. He always tried hard to keep me happy and I didn't appreciate it. That thought alone made me want to leave. He deserved someone who would appreciate him and be kind in return and who would respect his family. However, none of that mattered once Duane entered my life. Nothing and nobody existed when he walked into the room. Everything around him seemed to either go in slow motion or stop completely. The noise around him became mute and I heard nothing except whatever he was saying. My focus was truly on him. He had me hypnotized. I was in a trance and under his spell. I never felt that way about anyone before, not even my husband.

Later that same night, I did my usual grounds checks to make sure clients were following the rules. I could care less what they were doing though. I only wanted to see what Duane was doing. I saw him coming out of his car. When we approached each other, I asked him to come into the office around nine to help me with the laundry. He said he would be there. Of course that was a cover and he knew it. I actually did have laundry to put away but I could do that by myself. I just needed an excuse to get him upstairs alone with me. If anyone saw us go up there we had a great excuse so no one would suspect a thing. Duane was right on schedule. He looked very curious and excited as he watched me put a note on the door that stated I was on grounds and would return to the office shortly.

"Grab a basket and follow me," I instructed. Duane picked up the laundry basket and followed me into the cold and dusty attic. I pointed to where the basket should go. Once he placed it under the linen table, I gently grabbed his shirt sleeve and pulled him off into the corner. We couldn't stand by the table. The window exposed us to the entire smoke area. The corner was secluded from the world. Once we were hidden, I wrapped my arms around him and brought his lips to mine. There was no hesitation from him. There was no gawkiness either. You know when you kiss someone for the first time and the kiss turns out awkward because the other person kisses differently than you and you're not sure what to do? It was not like that with Duane. It was if we kissed a million times before. It was like this moment was meant to be or that it was waiting a lifetime to happen. Our tongues danced with each other in perfect rhythm. Our lips melted together and it made me weak in the knees. It was perfect and it felt so right. Duane got my body going like no man ever had before. I could feel my excitement moisten the inside of my shorts. I could feel his anticipation too. It was gently digging into my womanly area as if it were trying to break through the barrier of my clothing and enter the very spot we both wanted it to go.

As I kissed Duane, I rubbed the back of his head. He seemed to like that because his entire body leaned in closer as if he couldn't get enough. My lips crept to the hollow of his neck where I gently suckled while my hands explored his body. The whole time we were kissing, I told him I wanted this moment to happen since he got back. I told him I was worried he would freak out and tell people that I came onto him.

"No sweetie, never." he softly replied. "I've fantasized about you. I didn't want *you* to freak out on me. God, you're so beautiful."

"You know I'm married right?" I asked. I wanted him to know up front that this was not serious and I wasn't going to leave my husband.

"Yes I do." he answered. "And that's ok. We can have fun for as long as you want."

I also told him if he ever said anything to anyone about us that I would deny it all. I would then have to exit him. I didn't like threatening him but my career would be on the line. I would do what I had to do to protect it.

"I was hoping to fuck tonight." I breathed. "But my husband is coming home right now and I can't. We will figure out something. Maybe I'll have a night shift soon and we can meet up in the middle of the night."

We spent a few more minutes together but I had to get back to work. Medication time was at nine thirty and I was already getting a line of people on the porch. I could hear them complaining about how they had to wait because I wasn't in the office. Duane adjusted his shorts to hide his arousal. I followed him downstairs and let him sneak out the back door to avoid questions from anyone. I went about my shift as usual. I was in good spirits, smiling, and thinking about Duane of course. The clients were clueless as to why I was so happy and I think that turned me on more. It was exciting having a secret.

It was a long weekend. It seemed to drag on forever. I couldn't wait to get back to work so I could see Duane. He must have missed me too because he charted as soon as he was allowed to. Other staff was there so we had to play it cool. Rosie, our housing specialist, was in her office and the door was open. She could hear everything we said, so I slipped Duane a small note saying that he smelled good. It made him smile. I wanted to tell him more but I had to wait for Rosie to leave which should be any time now. The minutes seemed like hours until she finally left a little after five. While doing a grounds check, I asked Duane if I could have his phone number since his file didn't have one in it. He wrote his number down but asked me to throw away the evidence. I'm not sure why he would think having his number on a small piece of paper would be a big deal but I did as he instructed. I also slipped him a quick peck on his cheek before he walked away. Throughout the day, I texted him little messages about how I couldn't wait to play with him.

I wanna play now his text said back.

I answered *We have to wait until everyone goes into their rooms for the night.*

Ok see you tonight his text read.

That would not happen until ten that night. It was a shelter rule for all clients to be in their rooms at that time. If they were found outside they would get a write up. This rule was strange since medication time was from 930-1030 pm. Many clients used the medication excuse to get out of their rooms even when they were not planning to take anything. However, I hoped to have everyone who needed meds quickly get them so I could see Duane before the next shift showed up. Brenda, the staff member who worked the night shift, usually arrived early. She usually arrived about a quarter to eleven so there was not much time. I couldn't wait until ten. I had Duane come in again around nine, which gave us a half hour before the medication schedule. This time I took him down into the basement. We went into a small room where empty boxes and previous client's items were stored. There would be no time for sex. Instead, I pulled down Duane's dark cotton shorts and began pleasuring him with my mouth.

Duane was different than most men I had been with. Men are usually silent when they climaxed or they grunted quietly. Duane let me know the entire time what I was doing to him felt good. He quietly moaned here and there. He stopped me a couple times so he could tell me he wanted to do everything with me, not just this. He also let me in on a foot fetish he had. He kept rubbing the bottom of my feet and I watched his manhood swell each time he did so. As I lightly nibbled and licked on his shaft, he stroked my feet. I never had a man do that before and I was nervous. I didn't like my feet or anyone's feet for that matter. I personally thought feet were ugly. He was really into it so I let him continue while my mouth worshipped his manly domain.

"Do you like what you see?" he whispered.

"Your cock?' I teased.

He laughed quietly. I think it was unusual for him to hear someone of my status say the word *cock*. Social workers were supposed to be professional and not say such dirty words.

"Yeah." he hummed as he slid his rod between my soft lips.

"Yes I do, very much," I told him, taking another hard suck at his massive erection as I seductively looked up at him."It's a nice size. I'm curious how it would feel inside me."

As I stroked his length and sucked on the tip, his moans became more frequent. I knew he was getting close to cumming. With each second, his body was arching forward, and he needed to support himself up by holding onto a shelf. His moans got a little louder but he was doing well on keeping quiet. He let out a louder moan and I felt his excitement flow into my mouth. When he finished, I cleaned up the area as well as myself. I didn't want to leave any evidence behind.

He hugged me tightly afterwards and I will never forget the look in his eyes. There was a twinkle in them. One that I never saw before that moment and that I would never see again. In that moment, Duane looked truly happy. His smile was genuine. He grinned from ear to ear. Most men didn't do that either. They usually rushed off once they got what they wanted. Duane followed me back upstairs and I let him out the back door like last time. I went into the front of the office and took the *"be back soon"* sign out of the window. Duane was coming around the side of the building as I did this. We smiled at each other one last time before I went back to my work.

Chapter 4

Secrets

It was a few days before Duane and I could be alone again. We had short opportunities here and there to show each other affection. When I did room inspections, we would hide in the bathroom together to sneak in a few kisses and hugs. Duane often asked about my husband. He was curious what he did for a living and what his personality was like. I think he was worried what would happen if Dave found out about us. I told him the worst that would happen was he would leave me for cheating. Dave was not the type of guy to hunt another man down and beat him up for sleeping with his wife. Dave would definitely fight a man who tried to hit him though. He never started a fight but he would end it. I told Duane he had nothing to worry about. My husband was not the jealous psycho type.

Duane and I were always worried about being caught so we never got to spend too much time together. I always had to go back to the office and help other clients. If I were gone too long, I know they would tell my manager. And who knows, maybe they did. Looking back now, I'm sure Chad and the other staff members knew more than they let on but nobody ever asked about Duane and I. They always beat around the bush about it. I was not going to give up information. I kept them wondering.

Next to the shelter was a construction site for a future party store. Duane and I would meet over there from time to time. If we were going to get caught, it was best to be off shelter grounds when it happened. I could get fired for being inappropriate off grounds but my chance of keeping my job were better if we were somewhere else. One night, Duane and I met up behind the store. We were tired of waiting to have each other. All this foreplay had gone on long enough. It was time to take things further. As we kissed and touched each other, I could feel him swell with eagerness. I was also getting very aroused. My panties were soaked and I ached for him to pull them down so he could be in the very place we both wanted him to be. There was a throbbing between my legs and I knew it wouldn't go away until my desire for him was fulfilled. Duane turned me around so that my face was against the wall.

"You wanna fuck, don't you?" he taunted in my ear.

"Yes," I whimpered. "Did you bring a condom?"

"Fuck!" he whispered loudly. "The one time I fucking forget to bring it!"

He stopped to think for a second. The he continued unzipping his pants. "Don't worry," he explained. "I won't come in you."

He pulled my jeans down to my knees and went on taking his stiff rod out of his own pants. I stopped him. Not because I was worried about getting pregnant or a disease. It was because I had this crazy thought that if he didn't actually experience what I felt like inside without the barrier of a condom then it was not really cheating. I know that sounds stupid. But again, at that time, I was not having rational thoughts. I wanted to believe any silly excuse I could think of to justify the terrible thing I was doing to my husband.

"We are going to have to wait." I reluctantly told him. He did not look pleased at all. I had an idea. I told him to meet me in the office around nine again and we would go up into the attic. When nine approached, I brought Duane upstairs. This time I unlocked the door to another small room where we kept old client files, clothing, and extra blankets. I grabbed two small handmade knitted comforters and spread them out on the hard wooden floor. I lay down and pulled Duane on top of me.

"We don't have much time." I said. "But you can have me now if you want. I hope you brought a condom this time."

Duane nodded and pulled his pants down. As he was putting on the condom, I also slid my pants off, fully exposing myself to him. I was very nervous. I had not had sex with anyone other than Dave in over eight years. I was worried Duane would not like what he saw. Luckily, it was somewhat dark. The only that light shone through the window was from the streetlight across the road. Duane had finished putting on the condom. This was it. This was the moment I ached for. It was so moist between my legs that Duane slid in very easily. I cried out with pleasure at his first thrust. Then slowly, he began gliding in and out. I felt my womanly lips spread as he pushed his way into me. He was a lot bigger than my husband.

Although my center was extremely wet, I was also very tight inside for Duane's massive manhood. He looked deep into my eyes and stroked my hair as he thrust deeper and deeper. I wrapped my legs around his waist and kissed on his neck. I wanted him to take me hard. I think he thought he might hurt me so he was slow and gentle. There was no time for being tender. My frame was small but I was a lot tougher than I looked. I just wanted to be *taken*. I told him he didn't have to be gentle with me. He stopped a lot to see if I was okay. I was more than okay. I could hear people on the porch wanting to get in for their meds. I couldn't stand this. Duane and I needed to go somewhere to be alone so we didn't have to worry about how much time we had or who knew what. I couldn't get off with these pressures.

"We have to stop." I mouthed, not wanting to stop at all. I told Duane he could come, but I think he was having a hard time too. Sex is not very fulfilling when you can't focus on it. He pulled out and we got dressed. Being with Duane was difficult. It was forbidden and we never had time to spend together. Hard or not, it was obvious Duane and I had feelings for each other and couldn't stay away long.

We attempted to be together a couple days later. It was the first time I got a glimpse of how upset and disturbed he could be. That day when I arrived to work, my manager informed me that Duane had some pills he needed to check into the office. The pills were called *Thorazine*. It was often prescribed to patients with mental or mood disorders such as anxiety, manic depression, and even schizophrenia. It scared me a little bit. I knew Duane had issues but he didn't appear to be schizophrenic. His file from his psychiatrist didn't suggest this either.

When Duane came into the office several hours later to chart, he looked so sexy. He was wearing a nice knitted shirt and his hair was slicked back. He also looked angry and worried. His pupils were the size of dimes. When I looked into them, he didn't look like Duane at all. It was if I were looking at someone else. He told he figured I didn't want to see him anymore because he had to take pills. He thought I was going to end our *"thing."* As he signed his name in the charting book, he set the pen down hard, glaring intensely at me while he did this. The look in his eyes scared me. It also turned me on. His darkness was sexy. He put the pen down so hard, it was more like he threw it down and it bounced a little on the desk and landed by me. I told him I didn't want to end our thing. Looking back now, I should have. I didn't see how deep into the water I was getting.

I told him not to worry about it. This didn't change how I felt about him. If anything it turned me on. The more I got to know him, the more mysterious and dangerous he seemed and it made me more attracted to him. After he left the office, he kept texting me and asking if I were okay and if I still liked him. It was cute at first but it got annoying real quick. He also indicated to me that he waited all weekend to be with me again and if I didn't meet up with him, then I was lying about liking him. I didn't want him to think that and possibly get so angry that he caused a scene. I told him to come to the office after medication time so we wouldn't be interrupted.

Duane came in as instructed and we went into the attic again. This time we went into the packaging room located on the left side of the building. As soon as we were in the dark room, he grabbed me and bent me over the desk. He was in a hurry and fumbled to get the condom on. At the same time, he was pulling my pants down. It was if this was his only chance to be with me and he couldn't have me quickly enough. He tried to enter me from behind but the desk was an awkward height and it wouldn't work. He pulled me down to the floor and entered me from behind that way. As he thrust, he held onto me by my feet. I looked back at him and he had his eyes closed as he glided in and out of me. It turned me on seeing him having so much fun and pleasure.

"You look good back there." I breathed, rocking my body backward into each plunge.

"You look good too," he whispered, keeping his eyes closed and his head pointed towards the ceiling. Duane pushed my head down so the rest of my body was up in the air. He came down with his chest on my back as he continued thrusting. He wasn't as gentle this time. Nothing mattered to him at this moment. All he wanted was my body right now.

"So is this considered sexual harassment?" he breathed into my ear.

"If it is," I lustfully answered, "You can sexually harass me all you want…"

My answer made him chuckle. I loved his laugh. It was the same low sexy giggle he made while I was going down on him a couple weeks earlier. It was quiet and short and that's what made it stimulating. He flipped me over and held me in his arms like the first time we were intimate. He felt so good. I couldn't believe how excited he made me. Many would say it was because it was new and different. But nobody else ever made my body react the way he did. As much as I was enjoying him having his way with me, I realized it was almost eleven o'clock, which meant third shift would be there any minute.

"Duane," I whimpered. "We have to stop."

Duane didn't stop. He didn't care what I said. He wasn't hearing me. He just continued to ram me.

"Please Duane." I said again. "I don't want to get caught."

He stopped reluctantly but did as I requested.

"I'm sorry." I apologized, giving him a quick kiss on the lips. "I promise we can be together soon." Although I reassured him of this, he looked very upset as if I were lying. He looked hurt, as if he were being rejected and was about to cry. He went back to his room and I finished typing staff notes on the computer. Duane kept texting me for reassurance that I still wanted him. I didn't know how else to say everything was ok.

"We just need to find a place where we can be alone." I said. "But I have to go. Brenda is here. We will talk more tomorrow I promise. Good night sweetie."

Duane and I had another chance to be alone a few days later. I was off work at nine. I told Duane to meet me on Lynn Road, which was a dirt trail located next to the shelter. He met me there, hopped in my jeep, and we drove down about a half mile. I parked off to the side and he and I went into the very back of the vehicle. As usual we did not have much time. I had to get home to my family so we had to hurry. I told my husband I had an intake at the last minute so that would explain why I would be late. Duane had me bent over the back seat and took me hard from behind again. He pumped faster and let out a moan to let me know he was releasing himself inside me. This was the first time he was able to and he loved it. He was worried that I did not get off. I explained to him that I have to touch myself to come. It has always been that way. It had nothing to do with his performance. I also explained that when I have to hurry I can't focus on an orgasm. My body and mind had to concentrate.

Duane smoked a cigarette while I got dressed. He wanted to chat with me but I didn't have time. I told him I had to go home. My husband was most likely waiting for me. I hated lying to Dave. This thing with Duane was more difficult than I thought. Not only was I having inappropriate relations with a client but I was being unfaithful in my marriage. On the days I had sex with Duane, I avoided it with Dave. I had to make up excuses as to why I wasn't in the mood. I usually told him my stomach hurt or that I had very painful menstrual cramps. I would perform oral sex on him to keep him satisfied. If I didn't, then he would know something was going on. When I was home, I wasn't really home. I was there physically but my mind was elsewhere. My mind was on Duane and I. My husband sensed this and was starting to get suspicious and ask me questions. I was not sure how long I could keep this up.

Chapter 5

Into the Black

The day started out as any other Tuesday. I was at home with the kids while my husband was at work. It was around ten in the morning. I was waiting for the shelter bus to leave for town so Duane could call me. That was the best time for us to talk since staff was busy with other tasks. The chance of him being interrupted by anyone was low. We usually had to do most of our communication over the phone when my husband was gone and the shelter was practically empty. He called me right on time and the first thing he said definitely caught my attention.

"Ok," he began in his usual monotone. "Let's admit that this is more than just fun for us."

"What do you mean?" I asked.

Duane explained that if I were going to have my cake and eat it too, he was going to do the same. He meant that if I was going to stay with my husband and see him on the side, then he was going to see other people too. He admitted it really hurt him when I would go home to Dave every night while he stayed at the shelter alone waiting for my return. He said he found somebody else. Those words cut me deep and I felt like I was going to burst into tears. I asked if I knew her and he said yes. It was Katie, a woman who recently stayed at the shelter but was forced to exit for failing her drug test. I knew Duane and her were friends but I had no idea they were into each other. He told me he slept with her twice the night before, and doing so made him realize he had deeper feelings for me. When he tried to have sex with Katie, he had trouble getting aroused. At first he thought he was going impotent but she said to him, "There's nothing wrong with your dick. You have a girl and you love her. You're just feeling guilty."

"Why should I feel guilty?" he screamed at me through the phone. "It's like I'm cheating on you. And I'm not. You're married. I'm just the other guy and I hate being the other guy. You're married and you're still fucking him so I'm gonna fuck someone else too." We talked for nearly two hours about the plans for us. He told me he thought Katie was pretty but he didn't like her the way he liked me.

"When I'm with you," he breathed sincerely, "Nothing else matters."

Duane being with Katie had hurt me too and I started to cry. "Don't cry," he kept saying with care in his voice. I know I had no reason to. He was right. I was married. I had a life with someone else. We weren't together and we weren't in love. But were we? Otherwise why would it hurt so much? I had no right to be mad. He didn't cheat on me. He was single and he could be with whomever he wanted.

"Well this really hurts." I laughed as I sobbed. "But you're right. I'm not your girlfriend."

"But I want you to be!" Duane exclaimed.

He gave me an ultimatum. He was going to keep seeing me. If I didn't leave my husband though, he was going to continue seeing Katie. That hurt me more. I was worried he may fall in love with her if he kept seeing her. But why should I care? He was supposed to be *"fun."* He was supposed to be something I did on the side because I was bored with my own life and wanted out. He was right again. It wasn't just fun. My feelings for him were obviously

33

stronger than I realized. I told him I loved him and just wanted him to be happy, even if it meant not with me.

I thought about leaving my husband several times. He was a great guy but he came with a lot of baggage. There were issues that I thought were little and would subside over time. However, little things become big things when they are not dealt with. I wanted to be with Duane so I decided I would leave. I wanted to leave even if Duane and I did not end up together. I felt guilty for cheating on my husband so I needed to get out anyway. I couldn't do it right away though. I needed time to look for a place to live and save some cash. All day long, I thought about Duane and Katie. Sometimes it pissed me off. Other times I accepted it. I did not realize the extent of my jealousy until I got to work later that day.

Work was busy when I arrived. Most of the staff stayed over to finish their duties. I was not able to see Duane for a while. After the transportation bus dropped clients back off to the shelter, charting began. Duane did not come in the office. I figured he would want to see me. He knew I got there at three every day. After a couple hours, I saw him sitting in the smoke area goofing around with other clients. Work slowed down for me so I had time to do room inspections. I locked up the office and went out the back door. I purposely walked past the smoke area and said hi to everyone as I darted around the fence. I often went that way to do grounds checks. Duane said hi too and I could see he was offended that I didn't look at him and say it. I wanted him to know I was there. While I was unlocking the door to room three, he came around the side where there was a hidden trail that led to the back of the property.

"I thought you were going to our spot," he said. "Our spot" was the unfinished construction site at the store where we occasionally met up at so we could make out.

"Nope," I smiled, trying to act like the hickies on his neck were not bothering me. "I am just doing room inspections."

I started walking back to the office and he followed me. I couldn't ignore Katie's love marks anymore. I began to laugh sarcastically. "That's awesome," I mocked. "You've got hickeys...nice." Even though I was laughing he knew I was angry. He kept walking with me and tried to get me to talk. He stopped me in the driveway.

"I can't talk about this right now." I warned. Rosie was in the office and could see us outside. Some clients in the smoke area were looking at us too. I was trying to get it to look like the two of us were having a professional conversation but I knew my body language suggested otherwise.

"Well I want to." he said. "Because I can see how jealous you are." I could tell he was turned on by my jealousy. He told me before he wasn't used to women liking him. He said he wasn't a "player." He was flattered that both Katie and I were into him.

"Listen." he went on. "You can't be mad at me. I'm not in a relationship with you."

"Well that's good." I sneered. "Now you and Katie can live happily ever after."

Duane's face fell. "But I don't like her the way I like you."

As much as I wanted to talk to Duane about this, it was neither the time nor the place. I had to get back to the office. I hurried and walked away before he could say anything else. I knew he was worried and feeling bad. He shouldn't

35

have felt that way. I shouldn't have let him feel that way. I was too irritated to care. Even though he wasn't my boyfriend, the fact that he slept with someone else hurt me severely. Seeing the hickeys all over his neck didn't help either. He claimed he had trouble getting hard with her, yet it appeared he had a great time.

The rest of the night was a blur. Duane came in to chart finally and wanted to talk about us. But he had way more to say than that. His pupils were huge again and that angry face I seen before was back. For about forty-five minutes he went on about Brandon, who was another client staying at the shelter. Apparently Brandon was going around telling clients he was going to kick Duane's ass. Duane did not tolerate threats and was prepared to fight anyone who did so. Then he kept going on about the shelter's stupid rules. I tried to calm him down, which I thought I did. When he finally walked out of the office, he said he was fine. However, as I did grounds checks a few moments later, I was passing his room and heard screaming and a bunch of loud thuds. I opened the door and seen Duane punching the fridge. His roommate, Elijah, was watching television and looked freaked out.

"Duane," I approached quietly, "Do you want me to bring your medications to you?" I was talking about the *Thorazine*, which I should have brought down already. In fact, I should have given it to him when he was going on and on at me in the office. He said yes so I went to go get it. As I was pulling the medication out of the closet, the phone rang. It was Brandon.

"Hey Denise," he replied, a little out of breath and speaking frantically. "Duane just punched me about five times in the chest then ran across the street to the park."

"Ok," I calmly answered. "I'll call the police."

I had no intention of doing so.

"I already did." Brandon said hanging up.

Dammit, I thought.

I went outside to see if I could find Duane. It was too dark to see anything. I called his cellphone and it went to voicemail. The police were already pulling into the driveway. An officer stepped out and introduced himself. Then he began asking me questions. I told him he would need to speak to Brandon since I was in the office the entire time the situation was going on. Clients were walking the grounds trying to figure out what happened. I told them that if they had nothing to contribute to the report they needed to go back to their rooms or they were getting a write up and possibly exited.

Brandon went on to say Duane knocked on the door looking very angry and asked for the movies back he let him borrow. Duane apparently said he was leaving and needed them right then. Brandon said Duane punched him a few times in the chest and ran away. However, when the cop examined his body there were no marks. The cop thought it was odd but said Brandon could still press charges. Of course Brandon wanted to. According to the other roommates, they did not see or hear anything so there were no witnesses to back up either side of the story. I went back in the office to try to warn Duane that the cops were there. Before I could, my phone said I had a voicemail. It was Duane.

"I think I just fucked up." was all he said.

I tried to call him again. No answer. I went back outside and saw Duane being arrested and put into handcuffs. The cop was reading him his rights. Duane stayed calm and did not say a word. I told the officers that he may need his medication. I grabbed it from the office and attempted to give it to Duane myself but the police stopped me. After statements were made, everything quieted down. The clients went back to their rooms and I waited for third shift to arrive. I wanted to call Duane so bad, but I figured he couldn't accept calls right then anyway. Waiting was all I could do.

Chapter 6

Crazy in Love

I called the police station around 7:30 the next morning. I lied and told them my name was Danielle. That was the name Duane used when he talked to his friends about his *"secret lady."* We could have no ties to each other or my career would be ruined. That was how the fake name got started. The cops gave the phone to Duane and he was surprised to hear from me. He thought it was over and that I would never want to talk to him again. He was very calm and talked in a depressing, low tone. He was worried he couldn't go back to the shelter.

He didn't really have any other place to go except to a home owned by a woman named Kristen. She was also a former client who occasionally let people from the shelter stay in her one bedroom home. Usually those she let stay there had to do some favor in return. For example, a place to crash in exchange for food or paying the heat bill that month. It was very small and most people crashed on the floor. The cops were called there often over domestic disputes. There was also a lot of drug use. I knew it was not a good idea for Duane to stay there yet that was his only option if he couldn't go back to the shelter.

Duane's bail was set at two hundred dollars. I told him I would come in around noon and pay it. He was very relieved about that. He said nobody ever bailed him out before. He told me when he got his disability check he would pay me back. I didn't really believe that at the time. I bailed a man out of jail several years before and he also said he would pay me back. That never happened. Whether Duane would follow through or not, I still wanted to get him out of there. I really felt in my heart that he wanted to better his life. Doing so wouldn't be possible if he was locked up. When I paid the bail, I asked for a receipt but did not want my name on any of the paperwork. I said this was an anonymous donation.

Shortly after I paid the bail, I headed to work. I was very anxious to know when Duane was released. While at work, staff was discussing the details of the night before. They were weighing the pros and cons of the incident and if it were in anyone's best interest for Duane to return. It was decided that Duane would have to exit due to the damage to the fridge and also the altercation with Brandon. This upset me due to the fact that nobody really witnessed anything that Brandon said. It was also brought to staff's attention that Brandon was going around asking other clients to write incident reports stating that they heard Duane screaming and seen fists flying. Luckily nobody would help out because it just wasn't true. Nobody wanted to get in the middle of whatever issues were going on between Brandon and him.

Although Duane was denied entry back into our program, he was allowed to keep his car parked there until he got it legal. All of his belongings would be safe in the office. A short time later that day, I got a text from Duane saying he was at Kristen's. I had to tell him he couldn't come back to the shelter. I was somewhat relieved because now he wasn't a client. If word got out that we were having relations, it would only be frowned upon but I could still keep my job. The bad news was it would be harder for me to see Duane if he wasn't at my work every day. Nonetheless, we still wanted to see each other and I figured out ways to do so. It wasn't until that following Saturday that I could see him. My husband was at work until two in the afternoon and my son Evan kept asking to go to the skate park. This was convenient for me to see Duane. The park was close to his place plus it was boring watching my son skate for hours so this gave me someone to talk to. I missed Duane so much. We spoke on the phone and texted those three long days but that only made me more eager for his touch.

Evan and I packed up and headed to Gaylord. I texted Duane and asked him to meet me up there at noon. He said he would be there yet I was scared that he wouldn't show up. I know there were parties at Kristen's and that Katie was crashing there too, so Duane was probably hooking up with her. I also figured he would be too tired from partying late that he wouldn't wake up in time to meet me. I was so relieved when I saw him walking around the corner right at noon. I told my son that Duane was a friend that I wanted to talk with. Part of the time Duane and I sat on a bench, watching Evan skate with his friends. We chatted about the shelter, Brandon, my marriage, and all the things that were in our way and going wrong in our lives. We made sure not to show affection in front of Evan.

We took walks around town where we were able to hold hands, kiss, and pretend that we were a real couple and it was only us in the entire world. We drove to the elk park entrance and sat in my jeep so we could be alone. I gave him a blow job right there in the parking lot. It turned us on that we may get caught. People were driving through the park and walking by the vehicle but we were careful not to expose ourselves. A little while later when we were taking another walk around town, we went behind a motel where he asked me to suck him off again.

"Are you serious?" I teased. I couldn't believe he was ready to cum again. I gave him a sexy smile as I got on my knees, pulled down his shorts just enough to pull his manhood out and did as he requested.

A couple days later, Duane texted me to let me know one of Katie's friends, Crystal, said he could stay with her for a little bit to get settled. It was out in Frederic which wasn't too far. This only lasted a couple weeks. Duane never found out the real reason why she kicked him out. Or at least he never told me why. He thought it was because her husband, a truck driver who was on the road a lot, really didn't like the fact that Duane was staying there. Crystal said he was ok with him but I don't think it was. Or it could be that Duane and I told her who I really was, and it freaked her out. She lived in a house that in my opinion should be condemned. She also sold drugs. These two facts alone could have made her think I was going to report her to the state or Child Protective Services. She probably thought I was going to have her turned in for drugs since I was a social worker and I was mandated to report such activities.

Whatever the reason, Duane was deserted at the shelter. He had stopped in there to see if he could come back but was refused. At that same time, Crystal dropped off his stuff into the parking lot and said he couldn't come back with her either. "I'm fucked!" was all he repeatedly screamed to me over the phone. I was at the shelter at that exact moment for a staff meeting. I promised I would help him figure something out when I got out. The meeting was about an hour and a half. By then, Duane had gotten his car started and stopped at a small run down diner in Frederic. I met him up there and was trying to console him when my phone rang.

It was Dave.

"Why the fuck do you gotta lie to me?!" he screamed and hung up. He must have called my work and they told him I didn't work that day, although I told him I was. I texted back saying I would explain when I got home. Duane and I sat and had a cup of coffee while trying to figure out what to do next. His only option was to go back downstate. He was close to his ex's parents. They always let him crash when he needed it. He also had an option to stay at his payee Tim's house. Tim was crazy and always gave Duane a hard time about his choices, but at least it was a place to stay. I handed him a hundred dollar bill, which he refused at first.

"Your car might break down and this will come in handy." I said, not taking no for an answer.

As we said goodbye, he said something that was yet another alarm that should have went off in my brain. He had me write down my full name and said, "Don't worry honey. I'll find a way to stay close to you." With one last tight hug, he drove off onto the interstate. He was going to text me when he arrived at Tim's. Now I had to go home and lie to my husband once again.

When I got home, I explained to Dave that the reason I said I was working was because I was going to the staff meeting, which I was getting paid for. Then I told him Duane was a client who was kicked out of the shelter and needed help packing his stuff. I said I had to keep it a secret because we are not suppose to help clients outside of the shelter. It is against the rules and also shows favoritism. I told him I cared a lot about Duane and wanted to make sure he got home safely. Dave bought the story, or so he said. He told me he felt that there was more to my story and I seemed to care more about Duane then I was letting on. He said he loved me and wanted to believe me, but it seemed like we were drifting apart. I felt the same way but we were willing to work things out. I secretly still planned to leave. I was drawn to Duane like metal to magnet. I wanted to give up the great life I had and chance it with Duane. I just needed time to get situated. I truly loved my husband and cared for him. The last person I wanted to hurt was him. But I knew things were going sour with us and it was just a matter of time before we split up. That time came much sooner than I expected.

For the next couple of weeks, I communicated with Duane mostly through phone calls and texts. He was about three hours south so visiting him was not possible. I wasn't sure when I would be able to see him either. I missed him so much. Keeping him and I a secret was just as difficult with him being away as it was if he were standing in the same room with me. My husband was getting more suspicious. He knew Duane and I were talking but I assured him we were just friends. I know he wasn't buying it considering the fact I spent most of my free time chatting with Duane. He also saw how excited I got when Duane left me a text.

Duane was staying on the couch at his ex-girlfriends parents' house. Even though he and Amber broke up a year before, Duane had stayed in contact with them. He didn't feel very welcome though, at least not with Amber. Duane overheard her complaining to her mother about him staying there. He told me they were giving him a week to find other living arrangements. He wasn't sure what he was going to do. He wouldn't have any money for another three weeks. I remember he was constantly worried if I really wanted to be with him. He always asked if I were going to leave him.

"Do you really want to be with me?" he asked angrily one time over the phone. "Tell me right now because I can't take being hurt again."

I told him yes. I was just waiting to save a little money first. I was already looking at places to rent. My husband found this out by looking at the browser history on the computer. If that didn't already irritate him, he finally had it one day when he saw Duane was calling. I didn't want to answer it.

"Why won't you answer it?" Dave asked.

"I don't feel like talking to him right now." I answered.

"Well if he's just a friend, pick up the phone and talk to him in front of me." he said, handing over the phone.

I reached for it but hesitated. If I spoke to Duane like I didn't care about him, he would freak out and say so over the phone. Dave would then know for sure we were more than friends. There was no way I could pretend. I finally admitted to my husband that I did have feelings for Duane.

"I fucking knew it!" Dave screamed, kicking the couch on its side. "Did you sleep with him?"

"No" I lied. I couldn't bear to tell him the truth. "We've kissed though."

Dave looked really hurt now. "Well that's the same as cheating. You need to move out, and then you can be together like I know you want. I know you've been looking for other places to live. And he's only interested in you because he doesn't have a pot to piss in."

That got me thinking. I knew Duane's living situation wasn't the greatest right now, but I didn't think he was using me. If that were the case, why would he choose to be with someone who was married and whom Duane referred to as *"out of his league"*? If he were looking to be with anyone for convenience, then he would have chosen Katie. She was single. She didn't have her own place yet, but she did have a job and was working with the state to get housing. He could have chosen her. Instead he told her he was in love with me and wasn't interested in seeing her sexually anymore. I of course didn't explain any of this to Dave because it would just cause more arguments and questions. I didn't have the energy to do this right now. I was relieved for him to know the truth about Duane. Yet I felt horrible because I know I just broke his heart.

September 24, 2012

I signed my lease and moved in to my two bedroom trailer on Spruce Street. It was a small. Yet it was cheap, cute and the perfect size for my son and I. It was the only place I could find in two days. I didn't have all the money either. Dave fronted me the difference. He just wanted me out. He also helped me move some of the furniture in. He was going to give me some more once he bought new stuff. Evan was confused about why we moved out. I didn't really know what to say without exposing too much for an eleven year old to know. I simply said that sometimes things just don't work out between grownups. I was nervous about being on my own. I always had Dave there to support and help me through tough times. I was unhappy for a while but I know Duane was a huge reason why I wanted out.

I couldn't believe I was giving up my perfect life for someone I only knew for a couple months and who I wasn't ever really able to "be" with yet. I had no clue what was going to happen next. I know I was excited about not having to sneak around with him anymore. The plan was to meet up at a hotel downstate the weekend coming up. It was also Evan's birthday and he was going to spend it with his dad.

This made it convenient for me to get away for a couple days. I gave Evan a hundred dollar bill to buy whatever he wanted with it. I dropped him off at his dads' and took off for the three hour trip downstate.

I arrived at the hotel around two in the morning. Duane was outside his room smoking a cigarette. When he seen me pull up, he had the biggest smile on his face. We walked up to each other and hugged so tightly for several seconds as if this were the last time we would see each other. He brought me into his room and laid me on the bed. Finally we could make love without worrying about who was going to walk in on us. We had all the time in the world. Nobody else existed right now. It was just us. He shyly asked me if we could do it without a condom. I smiled and told him yes. He pulled out some restraints that he had in his storage unit. He mentioned them to me several times and he couldn't wait to get me in them. He was very much into bondage. I had never done anything like that before but was willing to try it. He tied both my legs and arms to the bed and took control of me. It was very exciting. Being helpless and vulnerable turned me on. After a few moments, Duane loosened one of the restraints so I could help him finish me off. That was what we did for those two wonderful days. We made love, took walks, went out for dinner, smoked some weed and had a couple drinks of rum.

The weather was beautiful that weekend, especially for being fall. The sun was shining and we didn't have to wear jackets. The breeze was a gentle one and it was so relaxing when it hit my face and had my hair blowing along with it. We stopped at his storage unit and grabbed one of his rifles and went to the gun range. He made a target board with Styrofoam cups and pinned them against a piece of wood that was hanging from a tree. He showed me how to aim and shoot the gun. It had a lot of power and it kicked me back when I pulled the trigger. It was exciting but scary. I was more comfortable watching him shoot. It was one of the very few times he seemed relaxed and peaceful. He loved being out there. I enjoyed watching him talk to other people who were out there that day. They chatted about their guns and tested out each other's ammo and rifles. It was very nice.

Later that night we were lying in bed. Duane had fallen asleep and was snoring quietly. I lay there in his arms wondering what was going to happen with us. I had to go back home tomorrow. His week was up at Amber's and he still had not told me what his next move was. Duane must have read my mind because he woke up and said, "I don't want to lose you again."

"What do you mean?" I whispered.

"I had to leave you once." he explained. "You're going back home tomorrow and I can't bear to see you go."

I didn't really want to leave him either but I had no choice. I had to get back to my life. He went on to tell me he didn't know where he was going to go. He was hinting on coming home with me. I told him he couldn't live with me but if he really wanted to start a life in Gaylord, he could stay with me a couple days until he got his disability check. Then he could use that money and find a room to rent until he could save and get something more permanent. He liked that idea. So that settled it. We would go to the storage unit in the morning and take as much stuff as we could and drive back up north. I was glad he was coming back with me. I didn't want to drive by myself. It was a boring ride alone. I wanted to be able to see him often whereas if he stayed in Hart I could only see him once a month.

I told him to be sure that he wanted to stay in Gaylord

48

for him. Not for me or for us since relationships often do not work out. I admitted I wasn't sure where this was going or if it would work out. He had to be sure he wanted to live there. He told me he was doing it for him as well but I never really believed that. He told me before he would find a way to be close to me. Therefore I knew I was the main reason he was moving up north. I didn't like being the sole reason. Here he was, moving hours away from any family or friends, to be with a woman who had just left her husband. It was a crazy idea. But it felt right. It felt like this was the way it was supposed to be.

Chapter 7

Good Girl

I called Dale, Evan's father, during the ride back up north. I was letting him know I was on my way to pick up our son. Dale suggested Evan stay with him this year. Evan was feeling uncomfortable and confused about the separation and the new house. He would rather stay with his dad where there was some familiarity. I didn't blame Evan for feeling awkward. A separation is never easy on anyone, especially the children. Although I was disappointed Evan wouldn't be coming home with me, I said it was ok and that I would see him on his next school break. This would give me time to figure out what I was doing and get settled in my new life. It would also give Duane and I more time to be alone. I definitely was not ready to introduce him as my boyfriend to Evan just yet.

We arrived at my place sometime after ten that night. I still had boxes of stuff all over the house. I had not found the time to move in yet. Duane brought in some of his stuff but kept most of it in the trunk. Neither one of us were in the mood to unpack yet. We spent our first night on Evan's twin size mattress that I laid out in the living room. We watched a funny movie as we dozed off to sleep. I was glad Duane was with me but I was nervous at the same time too. I could tell he wanted to move in but I wasn't ready for that. I was not willing to move out of a house with one man and quickly jump into a different living situation with another. I told him he could stay for a week and I would help him look for a place to rent. My landlord lived only two houses down from me. I was worried she was spying so I was upfront about Duane staying for a week. She said it was fine but he would need to pay her $50.

For that week, I went to work as usual. It took me about twenty minutes longer to get there from my new place. The drive was already a half hour. I had to leave even earlier to get there and I spent a lot of time commuting back and forth. The other moments I had away from work was to check online websites for places for Duane to rent. Most places exceeded his budget so we started researching rooms to rent. We were constantly calling and emailing to inquire about the rooms. It was exhausting. I wasn't in the best shape health wise. I felt terrible for what I did to Dave and I needed to process the separation. I had lost a lot of weight and I noticed some of my hair had fallen out in the front where my bangs were. I tried to be alone at times but it was difficult when Duane was always around. I tried to take a bath a couple times to think and cry but he would come into the bathroom and pressure me to talk.

"You know you can talk to me about anything." he offered.

That was impossible. Not when it was about Dave. The main reason I left him was because of Duane. It wasn't easy talking to my new boyfriend about my husband. I tried before. All I got out of it was his opinion and advice that was basically negative towards Dave. I couldn't wait until Duane would get his own place so I could have my alone time and deal with the feelings that I was bottling up inside. While I was at work, he took care of things around the house such as organizing, cleaning, and fixing stuff that I didn't know how to. I was used to Dave being there and doing all that. I never had to do things by myself. Duane was not as much of a jack of all trades as Dave but it was still nice to have a helping hand. We also had relaxing evenings listening to our favorite music while we drank wine and smoked joints. He would give me foot rubs that often led to sex or him touching himself while he rubbed my soles. He loved to touch my feet. If he saw them, he would grab one and either start tickling it fiercely or caress it. One particular time he was rubbing my feet and I started to get turned on and very wet. I unzipped my pants and started touching myself.

As I got closer to climaxing, I breathed. "Tell me I'm a good girl...."

"You're a good girl." he breathed as he massaged my soles and sucked on my toes. As he repeated the phrase, I started to cum. As my orgasm intensified he said, "You are *such* a good girl."

When I finished, he pulled my pants all the way down so he could get inside me and satisfy himself. From then on he called me his good girl or his "little fucky." He often called me these names while he held me down and tickled me. He liked to tickle torture. He would bind me up and tickle me to see how much I could take. It turned him on so much. He wanted me to do it to him too. Sometimes I did although it was new to me and I wasn't sure what to do. One time we were sitting on the couch watching a show and he grabbed me and began to tickle fiercely. I took control and pushed him to the floor.

I got on top of him and said, "Let's see how you like it!" I grabbed his foot and tickled it as hard and fast as I could. He really enjoyed that.

Sometimes when I was too tired to play, I would watch him masturbate. It was very hot. Sometimes he would stand up and rub one out. I would watch his juices shoot out of his shaft and onto the floor as he cried out in pleasure. I loved hearing him cum. Every other guy was silent when they got off. Occasionally they may grunt or breathe deeply but Duane made sure I knew it felt good to him. Other times he would lie down and masturbate and I would see his juice trickle out and run along the side of his cock and down onto his legs. I would help clean him up. Sometimes when he masturbated I would get turned on and masturbate right next to him. There he would tell me I was a good girl and that alone would make me cum just from hearing those words. Another time we were in the bedroom and he massaged my feet until I fell asleep. A little while later I woke and he was still touching them. I felt a vibrating sensation and I could tell Duane was masturbating. I didn't interrupt. I let him finish. I could tell he was coming because he moaned quietly, maybe as to not disturb me.

When he was done I asked, "Did that feel good?"

"Yes..." he breathed, grabbing a shirt and wiping his excitement off of his stomach. Then we fell right asleep.

Another game he enjoyed playing was cop and "drunk driver." He would pretend he had pulled me over for reckless driving and would inspect my entire body, especially my feet. He enjoyed pretending I was concealing drugs within my toes and he would ask me to spread them apart so he could see what I was hiding. To change things up, I often acted like the irate woman who insisted she didn't do anything wrong and begged to be let go. Sometimes he would let me go if I provided sexual services. Other times he whispered in my ear that my rude behavior had only made things worse for me. He would then throw me on the bed, tie my hands behind my back, and fucked me hard from behind to teach me that I needed to respect the law. Yet there were times when Duane would not get erect or stay hard. I asked him if it were me but he said sometimes his mind would think disturbing thoughts.

"Like what?" I asked.

"Being raped in the ass," he answered.

Say what? I thought. Was this something he was into? I didn't understand why he would think about that stuff when he was with me. Then he shared something very personal with me.

"When I was really young," he began, "I was molested."

"By who?" I asked. "Your parents?"

"My mom." Duane admitted in shame. When he saw the confusion and sorrow in my eyes he quickly continued. "Well. It wasn't exactly by her. She let people do it to me."

I shook my head in anger. "What the hell?!"

"She was really high when it happened." he went on. "Sometimes she didn't have money for drugs so she would let people do things to me in exchange for them. She knew it was going on but didn't stop it."

I felt so sorry for him. No wonder he was so angry half the time. He had been through so much. I held him tight while I asked him more questions. "How old were you?"

"About four," he mumbled.

"Do you remember it?" I asked.

He nodded slowly, "Vaguely. Bits and pieces."

I didn't ask for details of what happened. If Duane wanted to say more he could have. I wasn't going to pry, simply because the story was pissing me off and I wasn't sure if I could handle it. I had a son of my own and the thoughts of me letting people do sexual things to him broke my heart. I just held Duane and told him I loved him. If thoughts like that entered his mind while we had sex, I suggested thinking about happy things instead. I also told him sometimes weird thoughts entered my mind during sex and thinking about something else instead helped.

"Your mom sounds like a piece of shit." I said.

"She was an addict." he said, "I forgave her."

"Either way," I said, "I never want to meet her."

On the last day that Duane was allowed to stay at the trailer, he got a call from a man named Bill, who was renting a room out for $200 a month. The place was outside of Gaylord. The timing was perfect. We drove over to Bill's to meet him and check out the room. Bill was an older man who was laid off for the winter. He did construction and that time of year was slow in Michigan. That was why he needed a roommate desperately. He seemed nice but somewhat quiet. The room was a decent size. It would fit all of Duane's belongings, which wasn't much. We took everything but the gun. We kept that in my closet. I was nervous having it there, but Duane wasn't sure how Bill would react to it. Also, Duane was worried about me being by myself. He felt strongly about me being able to defend myself from intruders. He was constantly thinking someone was going to try to break in with me there. He said it happened to him once and that's why he got the gun in the first place. He made sure I knew how to operate it in case someone broke in.

Although Duane had his own place, he often stayed at mine. I was used to having someone hold me at night so being alone wasn't something I could tolerate long. He would stay for a few days then go back to his place when he had to take care of business in Gaylord. Sometimes we stayed in his room. He didn't have a bed so it was uncomfortable lying on his sleeping bag. I brought him a cot from the shelter but he never used the foldout part. He used the mattress to add more comfort to his sleeping bag. We spent most of the time in there playing cards, or watching television. We had to be quiet so Bill wouldn't get upset. I didn't like being cramped in that little room so we chose to stay at my place. I didn't have a bed either but I had a queen sized mattress that offered more comfort.

I had shut my life out from my friends because I was not sure how they felt about my separation and the fact I was dating someone with lots of issues. It didn't matter to me. The time Duane and I spent together was special to me.

While I was at work, Duane spent most of his time dealing with the court issues that involved the fight with Brandon. He was also having a hard time receiving his disability money on time. Tim, his previous roommate from downstate, was currently his payee. However sometimes it took Duane up to two weeks to get his money. He needed the money right away to pay his bills. I suggested I would be his payee. The nearest Social Security office was in Petoskey, which was about thirty minutes from Gaylord. On my next day off, we took a trip up there.

Instead of me becoming Duane's payee, something better happened. The clerk asked me how I felt about Duane's spending habits. I told her I felt that he was very responsible with his money. That was enough for her to make him his own payee. Duane was ecstatic. In seven years of receiving disability checks, he was never his own payee. This was a huge accomplishment and a cause of celebration. I was so proud of Duane. He was on his way to becoming more responsible and self-sufficient. He hugged me tight and told me I inspired him to do better.

He also tried to find work. He often ran into other clients from the shelter while he was job searching. He would get side tracked from chatting and hanging out with them and he wouldn't accomplish much. Then that would upset him and make him feel like a worthless loser. The next few hours he would ramble on about and it would get exhausting to hear. I felt like we argued about him finding a job, but he was the one who kept bringing it up that he needed one. Then he would complain that he didn't have one. I tried to help with prioritizing his day and gave him rides to places. If I couldn't drive him, I would give him money for the bus. He had a car but it was still downstate in Amber's driveway. I driving him around caused a lot of arguments too. My car was having issues and it was constantly going into the shop. The bills from the repairs were putting me in debt. I started requesting money from those quick payday loans. Those are the ones that credit money into your bank account within twenty four hours. They were convenient yet expensive. I had two weeks to pay it back. It would be taken right out of my account. I always paid on time but then I would be requesting more money to pay bills. It was a vicious cycle that I couldn't get out of. It was stressing me out and putting me in bad moods. I tried to explain it to Duane but he never really listened to me.

When he saw I was angry he thought it was about him. It was never really about him. I was worried about not having a car to get to work. I was also worried that if my car broke down then I wouldn't be able to see him or help him out. I texted Dave questions about the car but he would give me a hard time. He would text back comments like, "*Ask your new boyfriend.*" Or "*Can't Duane fix your car?*" The answer was no. Duane was not mechanically inclined and I wasn't used to that. In fact, he wasn't really able to do a lot of things other men in my past could. He was like an overgrown child. I wasn't used to supporting a man to the extent that I did. I really cared for Duane, but it seemed the longer we were together, the more I missed Dave. I felt like

Duane's mother more than his girlfriend. I was always mentoring him and showing him ways to do stuff. He was thirty years old. Most of the things we talked about were topics that a thirty year old man should know. I was seeing more of why Duane was on disability.

However, I couldn't walk away from him. I felt like he needed me. In some way, I needed him. He was all I thought about. I was worried that he wasn't taken care of and I was the only one who could and would be there for him. I was worried more about him than myself, and I definitely needed to still take care of myself. I put his needs before my own. Not only did I have my life to worry about, now I had his. I had doubled the problems to deal with. It was so exhausting. I didn't know how much more I could take.

Chapter 8

Disease

If things weren't stressful enough with Duane and everything in his life, he got a letter from the court saying he had to pay $435 by Christmas or he would go to jail. For a few days, that was all I heard him complain and scream about. He didn't have enough money for that, Christmas gifts, and rent money for Bill. I suggested he call the shelter and speak to Chad about coming back. Then he would be able to pay his court fines and have a roof over his head.

"Are they going to let me back there?" he kept asking me. He woke me up in the middle of the night a couple times screaming that question. I told him the same thing I always said.

"If you explain your situation and show you've changed," I explained, "They may let you back. All I can do is put in a good word for you. I can't make the call." I was tired of repeating myself. I would often pass out on the couch because Duane's midnight outbursts were disrupting my sleep. Not to mention he snored so loudly and often right in my ear. He loved to cuddle so I was often woken up to his loud snoring right by my head. I would move away or take his arm off of me to get some space. This upset him. It made him think I didn't want him around or love him. That was not the case. I liked to have my own space especially when it came to sleeping. I could never convince Duane enough that it wasn't about him. I did want him around. I wasn't going to leave him. He constantly asked me that. There were times I thought it would be best for us to break up. He would either get upset or sad. Then he would make comments about the gun.

"Well since you're breaking up with me," he said over the phone, "I'm glad the gun is at your house then." Threatening to take his life if I left him was starting to get old. It made me feel trapped. Parts of me thought he was bluffing. The other part scared me because I think he would do it. But trapping me in a relationship, saying he was going to kill himself if I left was unfair not to mention sick.

The next day, Duane called Chad and asked if he could come back. I was sitting right next to him listening to the entire conversation. Duane told him he got job at a restaurant but had not started yet, that he was his own payee now and that he had been renting a place but wouldn't be able to afford rent and pay court fines. He needed to pay the court and save money for a new place to live. Chad said he would speak to Meredith, the coordinator of our program, and he would get back to him shortly. When I got to work that day, Chad told me that Duane called asking to come back. I had to listen as if I knew nothing about Duane's whereabouts. He asked me how I felt about his return. I said it would be fine as long as he was respectful, followed the rules, and didn't become violent. Chad said the only person who had an issue with Duane's return was Rosie. However, from the looks of Duane's situation, he wouldn't need to be at the shelter long. He just needed another disability check and he could have enough cash to get a place. That was the only reason Rosie agreed on him coming back.

With the housing program, if a client puts in the first month rent and deposit, they could qualify for rent free housing for up to two years. Sometimes if the client didn't have all the cash, the housing center would pitch in some too. So on December 3rd, Duane told Bill he had to move out and he checked back into the shelter. So here we were again, the social worker dating the client and they had to keep it a secret. However, this time the "rumor" had gotten out and everyone was talking about it. Chad even asked me about it one afternoon. He said he knew it wasn't true, but still asked me. I didn't say yes or no. I just laughed at him and walked away. This time however, that meant eyes were on us and we had to be extra careful not to let our feelings show. It was more difficult than I had imagined.

When Duane first came back to the shelter, he was calm and very positive about changing his life and getting his own apartment. Everyone noticed a change in him, even Rosie. He made it to every meeting, both one on one and morning group. He charted on time every day. He was respectful. He kept his room clean. He had not started his new job yet but did have orientation there which he made it on time for that as well. Everyone could see Duane was trying very hard. We helped each other out too. He would text me when someone was entering another client's room. I text him when there was going to be drug testing. He got a prescription for Xanax that he shared with me when he came up for medication time.

Yes we were very inappropriate. It was a very disturbing relationship that I could not walk away from. Duane had mental issues and I should have known better. Perhaps I was the truly sick one. Nobody said anything to us but they knew something was up. They would look at us when we entered the room to see how we would react to each other. Duane and I just pretended that we weren't anything except a social worker who was assisting a client. I didn't like that I had to pretend he didn't matter to me or that I wasn't in love with him. It hurt but it was exciting too. We would wait until people walked away before winking or blowing kisses at each other. Duane would grab my foot from under the desk and massaged it as we charted. We wanted each other so bad but there was no time or place to go. I was able to give him a blowjob once while he was there. It was in the same little room that we went the first time we were alone.

"Does this bring back memories?" I teased while my mouth made love to his rock hard shaft. Not being able to hold me made Duane very upset. "I need to get out of here." he complained between gritted teeth. "I need *you*."

My body was getting very lonely for him. I was home alone one day and feeling very aroused. I pleasured myself with my hand and recorded my moans and sent them to him. My phone wouldn't let me video tape it so recording it was my only choice.

"Are you ready for me to cum?" I breathed into the phone. "Are you ready? Because it's coming...." I made a few recordings before sending my favorite one to him. A little while later he sent me one back whispering that yes he was ready. It was very hot. However, I wanted it to be for real. I wanted him here with me.

About a week before Christmas, Duane called me at the shelter and was very upset. He was at the doctors and said his blood test results shown possible hepatitis C. He asked me if I had it and if I gave it to him.

"I don't have hepatitis C." I assured him. "I've been tested but I can get tested again to prove it to you."

Duane was scared. He didn't know much about hepatitis C. Neither did I. His doctor was going to retest the blood to be sure. The test he took did not specifically say if someone had the virus. It only showed that the body had developed antibodies to fight it. Meaning, the virus was in him at some point but may be gone now. Unfortunately, whether someone has it or not, the blood test will always show antibodies. I reassured Duane that we would figure this out and handle whatever happened.

"Are you going to leave me now?" he sadly asked.

"Of course not," I said. 'Please try not to think about this too much. You're only going to worry yourself sick. And it's probably nothing. We won't know for a while. Let's just try and have a great Christmas."

Duane was never the same after that. When he and I tried to talk about other things, he often brought the conversation back to Hepatitis C. Him and I went on the computer to get information. I printed stuff out for him to look at in his spare time. Rosie sat down and talked with him about it too. I gave him an 800 number to talk to a specialist about. In the meantime, I went to the doctor to get tested. He asked why I thought I had it. I explained that I worked at homeless shelter where clients often have diseases such as these. I also told him that my boyfriend's blood tests showed antibodies.

"How long have you been dating?" he asked.

"It's been a few months now." I said. I also told him about my divorce and that Duane was someone I began dating after my separation. Of course I didn't tell him the whole truth. I couldn't handle more judgments from people. It was my business anyway.

"I think it's time for a new boyfriend," my doctor said while the tech took my blood. I laughed quietly although I wasn't sure if it were a joke. I think my doctor was only looking out for me. I could tell he felt bad. Not only was I going through a divorce but now the man I was dating could possibly have hepatitis and may have infected me.

"When can I have the results?" I asked on my way out of the office.

"Two days," he said. "But if you have been dating this man for only a few months, I would suggest getting tested again. Sometimes it takes 7-8 months for your body to make the antibodies."

This scared me. So my test could say negative and yet I may still have the virus. Then I would have to wait even longer to find out? I was so nervous. I don't think I slept much those next two days. If I were this frazzled, I couldn't fathom how worried Duane was. He was already a worry wart. His doctor was going to call him in a couple of days after retesting his blood. We would probably receive our results at the same time. That was what happened. I was at home waiting for my doctor to call back. I was getting very anxious. I could not wait any longer. I called the office and asked to speak to a nurse. I was only on hold for a moment but it seemed like forever. The nurse got on the phone and told me that they usually do not read results over the phone. I explained to her that I lived a half hour away and I didn't have the time or gas to drive all the way there to get a yes or no.

Finally, the nurse stated, "When results are positive we don't tell the patient over the phone." I didn't understand. She repeated the sentence. It took me a second but I caught on.

"So I'm ok?" I asked.

"Yes," I could vision her smiling on the other end. "If you were positive, we would have you come in."

"Thank you so much," I breathed deeply and hung up. I felt relieved. But now I was worried about Duane. He must have been thinking about me too because he called me within seconds of hanging up with the nurse.

"I got my results," he started, sounding frustrated.

"So did I," I said. I started to tell him my results were negative but he interrupted me to say his blood still showed hepatitis.

"I have it," Duane angrily replied.

"I'm so sorry hon," I told him. "What happens now?"

"They are going to have me see a specialist in Petoskey," he explained. "They will test me there to get accurate results and see how advanced it is."

There was still a possibly that he didn't have it. Only the specialist had the equipment to take such tests. I tried to explain this to him and keep him positive but he wasn't hearing me. I felt so bad that he may have hepatitis. He had already been through enough. He didn't need another negative thing on his plate. Although I felt bad for him, I was a little irritated that he didn't even acknowledge my results. I thought he would be happy it was negative but he didn't care. I didn't blame him though. I'm sure I would have been devastated if my doctor told me I had an almost always fatal virus. I couldn't shake the idea that he was pissed that I didn't have it. It seemed like he was hoping I did so that I was guaranteed to stay with him. I know he was worried I wouldn't want to be with him because of this.

Chapter 9

Tempest

After Duane had received the news that he may have hepatitis, he could barely speak of anything else. He kept calling the 800 number and asking questions about the disease. That was a good idea because he needed to know how to live with it. Hepatitis is not a death sentence. Yes, most people who are diagnosed with it eventually die from it. However, most of them still led long and fulfilling lives. Eating properly and getting exercise had a lot to do with the progression of it. Also, not drinking alcohol or smoking cigarettes had an effect as well.

Couples could have a healthy sex life if they took precautions. It was better to use a condom but as long as there was no blood or a way for it to get inside a person, the virus could not be transmitted. Sometimes Duane and I used condoms. Sometimes we didn't. I knew I was taking a huge risk with him but I loved him and wanted to prove that it didn't matter to me if he had hepatitis or not. I just wanted him around me. However, he was afraid he was going to give me the virus so we didn't have a lot of sex after that. Duane still had his urges to get off but I could see a huge difference in his sex drive with me.

I tried to keep Duane busy with tasks to keep his mind off his health. Until he could see a specialist, he wasn't really going to have answers. He went on about his day looking for housing with Rosie. He also went to orientation at his job.

His first actual day of work would be on the seventeenth of December. He also went Christmas shopping for me one day. He felt bad because he wouldn't have enough money to get me much. I said I didn't care. All I wanted for Christmas was him spending it with me and Evan. He filled out an overnight pass at the shelter. He asked for three days, which was the most a client could ask for before they were considered exited from the program. Duane was upset because he was told by Chad that he may not get those days off. Monica, the case manager, was not very fond of Duane. She felt he had not earned the right to leave for the holiday. Apparently he had been giving her problems when they had their weekly meetings. She was not thrilled with him being there in the first place. She also didn't think he was following rules. She believed the rumor of us to be true and that he was really spending the holiday with me and not his family in which he claimed. She was right but where was the proof?

I thought it was interesting for her to act like that considering she was dating a previous client as well. Monica was a lesbian who had befriended another lesbian client a couple months before. Although this anonymous client had more time to stay at the shelter, she had exited early so she and Monica could be together. Monica thought she was being sneaky. However, everyone saw her car parked at the same exact resort that this client was staying at. They were also seen driving around town. I often passed them on the road. Her client would cover her face with a hoodie but I could still tell who it was. Therefore she had no right to judge when she was doing the same thing.

At first Duane's overnight pass was denied. However, after Chad spoke with her about the importance of Duane having his "family" around, Monica had a change of heart.

Besides, who really should be at a homeless shelter on Christmas? Some clients had nobody so there was no choice but to stay there. If a client had someone who wanted them around, that client should never be denied the right to go spend time with them, no matter the circumstances. Duane was not scheduled to go back to work until a couple days after Christmas, so his pass was approved for December 22-25. He was to return by 5pm on the 26th.

On the night of December 21st, sometime in the wee hours of the morning, a huge storm began that covered most of northern Michigan. I was alone in the trailer when I woke up to the sounds of high winds. The wind was so strong the trailer shook to the extent that I thought it might blow over and crush me. Then the power went out. I was so scared. I couldn't see anything inside or out. I used my phone to light my way to the kitchen to find some candles. The battery on my phone was almost out and I couldn't recharge it. I got the candles lit and turned off my phone to save the juice. Despite the scary blowing of the wind and the shaking of the trailer walls, I managed to fall asleep.

I woke up a little while later and turned the phone on to see what time it was. It was a little after three in the morning and I had a call from Duane. He left a voicemail saying the power at the shelter was out and clients were allowed to find shelter elsewhere until it came back on. Families with children were given a motel voucher to a local motel that still had their power on. Duane said since staff didn't care what clients were going to do, he was allowed to start his overnight pass tonight and that would give us more time to spend together. I texted him back saying the power was out and my phone was going to die. I would contact him tomorrow when I was able to charge my battery.

I woke up early the next day to see the devastation outside. Trees were down everywhere and my car was buried in the snow. I couldn't even begin to estimate how many inches of snow we got. I went outside to start shoveling my car out so I could drive to work later. I had several hours before I had to be there but I knew shoveling was going to take that long. When I went outside it was eerie quiet. I heard nothing from any of the neighbors. Nobody was outside shoveling. I shoveled a few feet at a time but had to take breaks. The snow was heavy and shoveling for a few minutes felt like double the time. Luckily, a man in a plow truck stopped by and plowed the end of the driveway so I could back up my car.

I was late getting to work due to the roads not completely being plowed yet. The office was toasty warm from a generator that the maintenance man brought from home. The clients were allowed to watch television in the community room during the day to stay warm. At 10 pm they had to go back to their rooms. I felt bad for them. I wanted to let them all sleep inside to stay warm but they wouldn't all fit. I felt guilty that I got to stay in the warmth while they froze in their rooms. Chad let me know that the power was probably going to be out for about three days. He also told me that Duane was on an overnight pass for Christmas.

As usual, I just nodded and acted like I wasn't aware of where he was really going. Duane messaged me later saying where he was at. He had been attending a local church and befriended an older couple who had recently had a baby. They said I could take a shower and get something to eat when I arrived. They even offered us to stay there until the power came on. It was a nice gesture, and although my house was beyond freezing, I needed to go check on it and make plans on what to do with Evan. I also felt awkward since I didn't know them and they had a very small apartment.

After I showered and ate, I thanked the couple for their hospitality then drove back to the trailer with Duane. Unfortunately, the power was still out. Duane and I went into the bedroom and covered ourselves with several blankets. I thanked him for coming home with me to my igloo even when he had the chance to be warm where he was. It was greatly appreciated and it was yet another thing he did for me that showed how much he cared. It was a little gesture that meant the whole world to me. We made love under the blankets for the first time in weeks. Outside the blankets felt like Antarctica. But underneath them the fire between us was burning brighter than ever.

A couple times, the blankets came off as we messed around and we didn't realize it until Duane had entered me. The subzero temperature in the house made his cock feel extra warm inside me. It was almost like I was burning up. The skin around my core was silky wet but the cold air dried it quickly. Yet when Duane slid slowly into me and then slid back out, his manhood was dampened once again from my excitement. The heat that generated from both of us that was quickly taken away from Mother Nature's bitter cold was such a turn on. While the rest of our bodies endured the below zero temperatures, Duane's cock was on fire and it took the chill right out of me.

He flipped me onto my stomach, straddled my legs and used them as a seat. As he rested himself on the back of my legs, he pumped harder and faster as I cried out with pleasure. I came very quickly for not having him in what seemed like an eternity. Now that I had climaxed, it was his turn. He continued to thrust as the juices from within me covered his shaft and my core muscles had tightened so much they gripped around his cock and didn't want to let go. When he slid out, they tightened around his head and demanded he get right back in. Duane's breathing quickened as he lunged harder and faster. Then he just stopped. I thought something might be wrong. As I turned around to ask him if he was ok, I was cut off by the loudest and longest groan I had ever heard from a man. He was looking up towards the ceiling with his eyes closed while remaining completely still inside me as he released himself within.

"Aaahhhh......" he cried out, with his hands calmly resting on his legs, and the rest of his body clenching while his juices filled me. It turned me on so much. I instantly got wetter. Most men, including Duane, would continue thrusting hard and fast as they came. For him to stop and sit completely still even past the moment of coming inside me was beyond sexy. I wanted more. My center was throbbing for pleasure. But I would have to wait. When he was ready, he would grab me and have me the way that he wanted. I loved his dominance. I loved succumbing to his every need and desire. It pleased me to please him. All he had to do was tell me what he wanted of me and I did it. He had complete power over me.

When Duane and I woke up the next day the power was still out. We were so cold that our skin had a stinging pain. I couldn't stand it. I had to pick up Evan but I wasn't going to if I didn't have lights or heat. I called my friend George in Mio and asked if he had power. He did. He offered for us to stay until the heat came on. I waited as long as I could to pick my son. He called on the 23rd and begged I come get him. He was excited about his Christmas gifts. George said he could stay there too and if we had to spend the holiday there that would be fine.

Occasionally, Duane would text some friends and ask them if the shelter's power had come back on. They said not yet. I figured we were all part of the same power line and if they didn't have lights yet then I most likely didn't either. I picked up Evan and came back to George's. We spent Christmas Eve there. We made a small dinner. It was nice yet I wanted to go home and let Evan open his gifts. I was excited for Duane to open his as well. On the 24th, I told George I was going home to check the lights. He said we were all more than welcome to come back if the power was still out.

Luckily, the power was back on. It was still very cold in the house though. I told George everything was fine and thanked him several times for letting us stay with him. I told him if he wasn't going anywhere for the holiday, he was welcome to have dinner with us. He must have busy because he never came over. It was just the three of us. My brother was supposed to visit but he got tired of waiting for the power to come back on. He sent me a message saying he would just spend the holiday with mom. The next couple of days were very nice. We opened our gifts and ate a nice ham dinner.

Duane and I got each other the same gift, the newest *Def Tones* cd. It was actually very funny getting each other the exact same thing. He also got me a zebra striped wallet purse and a very nice card with a long and loving message in it. It was a sad letter too. I wouldn't really understand the meaning behind it until later. I remember watching him write it a couple weeks earlier while we were sitting at the dinner table. I was busy going over bills while he sat across from me to write the letter. He looked so sad as the pen wrote away. He looked like he was going to cry. I figured he was involved deep into what he was trying to tell me and it made me smile. I got Duane a few more gifts then he got me and it made him feel worthless again. I told him I didn't care about getting lots of presents. I was just glad he was there with me.

Duane went back to the shelter the day after Christmas. His first day of work was the following day. Rosie also said he was expected to exit into his new apartment any day now. After I dropped Duane off at the shelter, I went back with Evan. I didn't have to work for another couple days. Duane's first day of work went well. He worked the next day but then didn't have to work until after the New Year. On December 29th, he received the key to his apartment and I started helping him move in. I let him pick out anything he wanted from the shelter basement and attic. He collected dishes, blankets, and common household supplies.

We grabbed a bed from the garage and I brought a couple things from home that I didn't need such as a card table, chair, and a stand for his television. We piled it all into the shelter van and drove to his new place. I had to hurry since I was still on the clock. It wasn't good to leave the property long. That was when the clients broke the rules since there was no authority there to watch them. I hugged Duane tightly before I walked out saying I was proud of him and he was finally free to live his life the way he wanted to. He worked so hard to change his life. I thought things were only going to get better. However, things were never further from the truth. Everything he worked hard for only started to go downhill after that.

Chapter 10

Bad Romance

Things seemed to be better once Duane finally moved into his apartment. I would stay the night there if I had to work early the next day. It saved me money on gas. Duane still came home with me sometimes. It seemed like he was afraid to be alone. Sometimes he begged me to pick him up. I enjoyed Duane's company, but I really needed alone time. I enjoyed my "me" time and I never really got that with him. I still didn't really get to process my separation from Dave.

However, Duane was upset when I didn't want to come over. He thought I didn't love him anymore. He thought I wanted to leave him, especially because of the hepatitis. He had an appointment at the end of January to see the specialist and finally find out if he even had it. We went around and around about the disease. He didn't realize he was pushing me away when he did that. I tried to stay away just so I didn't have to constantly console him. He worried himself sick every day. I couldn't take it. I was losing my mind, my hair, and my appetite.

We began to fight about everything. Then we would make up. We would apologize for misunderstanding each other. This happened over and over on a daily basis. Sometimes it would happen several times in one day. We spent more time arguing than anything else. It was becoming a lot of work just to communicate with each other. We decided we should take a break from our relationship.

However, our "breaks" never lasted long. We would end up spending the night together. It was very confusing. When we were together, we couldn't wait to get away from one another. Yet when we were apart, we longed to meet up again. Not every moment with Duane was irritating. We still had great times. We would cuddle and laugh at the goofiest things. Stuff that other people would think was dumb. I never felt so me when I was with him. It was like he got me. I don't understand how I could fight with someone about not understanding me yet there were times when he was the only one who did. I would wake up in the morning and he would tell me how beautiful I was. I didn't have to put on makeup or do my hair for him to see the beauty in me.

My car continued to have problems. When I first took the car in it only needed a ball joint. Then over time it needed more repairs. I did not have enough money to keep getting it fixed, so I continued to battle with the payday loan issue. I was so stressed about it one day that I started to cry. Duane held me and said it was my turn to lean on him for help. He was going to draw out his disability check and give it all to me. I was to pay him back a little over each of my checks. However, just a few days after he loaned me the cash, he was upset because he didn't have money to buy what he needed.

The fighting got worse. Duane was growing angrier. I wasn't really sure why. Every day it was a different reason. It was usually about hepatitis. He said he wouldn't be beautiful anymore. He was constantly worried he would give it to me. He would stand in front of the mirror for a long time after shaving to make sure he didn't have any cuts on his face. He was worried the blood would get on surfaces and possibly transfer it to other surfaces or other people. He inspected his body for open wounds and made sure I didn't have any either.

I was glad he was being cautious but it was now beginning to become an obsession. It was the center of most our conversations. I was tired of hearing it. I know he was worried but he wasn't going to know anything for sure until his appointment. I tried to keep his mind on other things. Sometimes I was successful. Other times I was not, especially if we were just sitting there in bed watching television. His mind was his own worst enemy. I understand now why he hated to be alone. People often ponder the most when they are alone. Thinking leads to the inventions of problems that never existed in the first place. With Duane's mind, there were always problems.

Duane would go to work every day and come home complaining that his managers were "punk bitches" right out of high school. He told me they acted like they were superior just because they were in charge. I know it bothered him that he was thirty years old and worked at a fast food restaurant. He felt like he was the one who should be ordering them around. I could empathize with that. I've had bosses younger than me and it did get under my skin. I explained to Duane that nobody was better than anybody else and they have been there longer and that's why they moved up. I told him if he stayed there long enough I'm sure he would move up to.

Either way, that was another thing that bothered him and he often vented loudly to me about. I started feeling like I was his therapist and not his girlfriend. I wasn't a very good therapist either. When Duane and I first got together, it was easy to calm him down and help talk about whatever was bothering him. Now it seemed like it made me angry and I started yelling back. Then neither one of us was calm and it ended with me packing my stuff and leaving. Then the negative texts and calls would start.

"Maybe we should take a break." I suggested a few times.

"You mean break up?" he would ask.

"No, not break up." I explained. "Just step back and spend less time together since all we do is fight."

He would say ok but then he would call or text a couple hours later begging me to come over. Of course I would say yes. I felt like I was abandoning him if I didn't. Everyone abandoned him in his life and I didn't want to be part of it. I wanted him to know I loved him and I wasn't going to walk out of his life. I told him several times that no matter what happened with us, I would always be there for him and want to know how he was. But he didn't just want to be friends. I don't think I could only be his friend either. Fighting or not, we were drawn to each other for some reason. One time I tried to break up with him and he said, "I can't go through this alone." He meant the hepatitis. He also mentioned that I was the only one who cared about him and he couldn't handle me leaving.

He was wrong. People did care about him. He just made it hard for them to get close. He would take the littlest things to heart and flip out on people. They were scared of him. He was sensitive and his heart broke too easily. He often put these negative thoughts into his own mind. People were not trying to hurt him like he thought. These thoughts caused him to scream and break stuff until they gave up. I was starting to give up too. I didn't want to though. There was a loving side to him that I fortunately got to see. Most people never got to see that. That part of him was the Duane I admired and became like a giddy school girl. That was the Duane that gave me the butterflies in the stomach feeling.

However, lately, the angry side of him was popping out more and more. Whatever depressing pool he was swimming around in, I started swimming in it too and was slowly beginning to drown. Duane barely touched me anymore. He worried he would give me hepatitis. I told him I loved him and was willing to take the risks. One day his finger was bleeding and I told him I was going to lick the blood to prove I didn't care if I got the disease. He stopped me. Luckily he did. I wasn't in my right mind. I was about to do something foolish and crazy for him. I wanted to prove that I loved him for him and I would still be there, although part of me was wishing the relationship would end. There was no way out. No good way that is.

January 11, 2013

It was about three thirty in the morning at Duane's apartment. I had the weekend off and planned to spend it with him. It was a nice evening for us, which was rare. We actually held each other all night. There was no fighting. No snoring in my ear. We fell asleep in each other's arms. I woke up in the middle of the night to use the bathroom and he was still holding me. It was so relaxing and sweet. I lay back down and fell asleep in his arms. That moment I will cherish forever. I was seeing the pleasant side to Duane, the one that got me hooked in the first place.

Now it was five thirty. Duane wasn't in bed. I got up and found him in the bathroom getting ready for work. I forgot that he had to be there at seven. He was dressed in his work uniform. He looked so cute. He was picking up towels off the floor when he looked up and his eyes met mine. Then I saw the beautiful smile that I adored so much. Then my mind went to a dirty place where I was visualizing I was a customer at the restaurant and he was taking my order. However, I wouldn't want fries with that. I would want some cock. I giggled quietly to myself at the thought. I hugged and kissed him, telling him he looked handsome in his uniform.

"Do you want a ride to work?" I asked, holding him tightly.

"No sweetie." he answered, holding onto me even tighter. "I can walk. You just go back to sleep ok?"

I nodded. His work was only a couple blocks away. I would have let him take the car but he still had not gotten his license back. Also, I had a distinct fox racing sticker on the back of my car and people would know it was mine. Although Duane was no longer at the shelter, he was still Rosie's client in the housing program. We still had to be discreet in our relationship. Duane left for work and I went back to sleep. He wouldn't be getting out of work until five in the afternoon. It was a long day waiting for him. I didn't have any errands to run. His apartment was pretty much clean so tidying it up didn't take too long. I watched some movies but they were the same ones I watched with him a hundred times before. I was bored. Not to mention extremely horny. I was hoping we could make love when he got back. It had been a few days and I needed a release.

A short time later, Duane texted to say he was on his way home. I asked him if he needed a ride and he declined. It was storming out and I felt bad he was walking in it. He insisted I wait there. When he arrived, I was laying on the bed watching television. He didn't have any other furniture so it was like a couch for us. It was a twin-size bed that we both hardly fit on, but it was better than the sleeping bag on the floor. He came into the bedroom to let me know he was there. He stood at the end of the bed talking to me. I sat up and inched my way to him. I looked up and asked in a sexy and innocent voice, "Can we have sex?"

He was surprised at my question yet intrigued at the same time Duane's eye twinkled and he answered, "You want to have sex?"

"Yes please." I nodded. I unzipped his pants and put his massive shaft in my mouth. He was erect already. He stopped me and gently pushed me to the head of the bed. We took each other's clothes off and he lay on top of me. Neither one of us wanted much foreplay. He entered me quickly and started thrusting. He would pull out far enough to where only the tip was inside me. He would wait there a few seconds and then quickly thrust back in. He repeated that, very slowly pulling out so I would feel every inch of him. Then he waited a little bit before pushing down deep again. With each thrust, I moaned louder each time. The anticipation was turning me on. I couldn't take it. Just when I thought he would glide back in, he would trick me and wait even longer before doing so.

It was amazing. I couldn't get enough of him. I couldn't get him close or deep enough. He made my body squirm and shake. My mind and body spiraled further and further into a trance. He was always trying new things with me. He was a different lover than anyone I had ever been with. We explored so many new things together. I learned a lot about myself from Duane. This was another one of those moments that attracted me so much to him. This was the Duane that made me forget about everything wrong in my life. This was the Duane that I couldn't live without. This was the Duane that made time stop. The Duane that had me under his spell and hypnotized me into doing anything he wanted. This was the Duane that made me weak and powerless. This was the Duane that I loved. He opened up a whole new world to me.

That night was perfect. That was also the last time we would *make love*.

Sunday came. Duane was scheduled to work early again. I would wait for him to get home and then we would drive to back to Lewiston. Duane and I both didn't have to work until the following Tuesday. He came home with me so we could feel more relaxed. When we stayed at his place in Gaylord, we had to be careful when we went out. We still didn't want people seeing us together in fear there would be repercussions. At my place in Lewiston, nobody from the shelter was there. Nobody knew us so we could be free with our relationship. Plus there was more to do at my place.

At my place, Duane was upset at some mail he had received. He got a letter stating he would be losing some state benefits because of his job and that he didn't report the changes in a timely matter. This made him very irate. He was shaking his fist in the air as he read the letter. I told him to call his caseworker on Monday. They just needed to update his information. It was a simple solution. With Duane, there were no simple solutions. He would worry himself sick about it until he could handle the issue. Unfortunately, I was the one who had to be there to deal with it all.

Chapter 11

I love you, I hate you

JANUARY 14, 2013

I woke up to the sound of someone knocking at my door. It was Dave. He had come over from the Atlanta Courthouse where we were scheduled to finalize our divorce. I didn't show up because he told me I didn't need to. As I came out into the living room to open the door, I noticed that the couch was pressed up against the knob so people couldn't get in. Duane must have done so before going to bed last night. This wasn't the first time he did this either. Once I asked him why he was paranoid about people coming in.

"I did some very bad things and I don't want those people that know that to find me." was all he said.

Since I knew Duane had mental illness I figured it was just one of his hallucinations. I never pressed him for more information but now I wish I had. Would he have told me the truth? I'm not sure. Sometimes I wondered if Duane knew what was true or what were fabrications in his mind. I moved the couch out of the way and opened the door for Dave. He needed my signature to sign off on the house and other assets. Since I told him I didn't want anything, he would only need me to sign some documents. I told Duane I had to run to Atlanta and I would be back soon.

Dave drove me there and I signed off on everything. It was a sad moment for me. It was then I realized that we were officially over. It was a chapter in my life that came to an end. A new chapter was starting and we both needed to turn the page. We both said we were sorry that it didn't work out for us. He dropped me back off at home. Duane was sitting at the table rolling cigarettes and he was irritated as usual. At first I thought he was jealous that I was with Dave. It turned out he was worried that he may have left his oven on. Now I had to drive all the way back to Gaylord to make sure the oven wasn't on and that there wouldn't be a fire. I sat at the table while he screamed about it. I tuned him out, put my head in my hands, and wept. I was sad about Dave. I still had feelings for him and I missed our life together. Duane didn't care. He didn't acknowledge my feelings. All he was worried about was his apartment. I had a feeling that he never even turned the oven on and that we were driving all the way over there for nothing.

I didn't want to drive. I wanted to stay home and sulk in my sorrow alone. But I also knew we had to check and make sure the oven wasn't on. All the way to Gaylord Duane bitched about how his landlord probably thought he was stupid for leaving the oven on. When we got to his apartment, the oven wasn't on but there was chicken in it. He must have gone to cook it and got distracted. *Great, now the mystery is over* I thought to myself. I wanted to go home. Duane begged me to stay. He seemed calmer now and apologized for this ranting. It was an everyday thing though. I wasn't in the mood to see anyone. I just wanted to go home and lay around in peace.

However, I felt like I was abandoning him so I stayed. I brought a new movie with us and we watched it. We also had sex but there was no connection. He was there physically but not mentally. He seemed off, like he was elsewhere. There was no love in his touches. It was as if he was only doing this for the physical gratification of it. Sometimes he felt he had to get off. This was one of those times. It took him forever to come. When he finally did, he seemed upset. He went to the bathroom to clean up while leaving me in the bedroom wondering if he even liked me anymore. *Why am I here?* I wondered. *What are we doing?* Duane came back into the bedroom and smoked a cigarette. We chatted about this and that but it was weird. I wanted to leave. He insisted I stay.

"It doesn't even seem like you want me here." I told him.

"I do sweetie," he insisted and lay down with me. We snuggled the rest of the night until we dozed off. The next morning he was getting ready for work. I told him I had to go home since I didn't have any clothes for work. I kissed him goodbye and told him I would see him after work. He asked if I could bring extra clothes with me so we could spend the night together.

"Sure," I smiled, even though inside I didn't really want to. Duane and I needed time apart. We were fighting daily. When I suggested we take a break, he would freak out saying I didn't love him and I was going to leave him. So I kept my mouth shut and pretended like everything was ok. I was worried he may actually hurt himself if he got mad enough. One time he asked me if I was only with him because I thought he would hurt himself if I left.

"No," I lied.

"Right," he said. "Because I won't. You don't have to worry about me hurting myself. If you don't want to be with me, then say so."

I went to work later that day but never went to Duane's. I told him I wasn't feeling well and just wanted to go home. He didn't like the sound of that but he said ok. I stopped by for a few to get his laundry and some bedding to wash. He didn't have a washing machine or money to go to the Laundromat. I said I would bring them over tomorrow before work. I stayed up late washing his clothes. I was upset. For one, I didn't get home until midnight every night. And for two, now I had to stay up later to do his clothes since I wouldn't have much time to do them before work. I was beyond exhausted. I missed my life with Dave. He helped me do daily tasks. It was not that Duane didn't help me because he did. I was just always running around doing errands for us both. I was exhausted. I missed the life I had where both partners did the running around to help each other out. I still loved Dave. I loved Duane too. Yet I think it was a different love. I'm not sure if I was in love with Duane. I know I never felt the same way about the both of them. I know Duane made me feel differently than any other man had in my life. All these thoughts were pissing me off and making me negative. I felt like Duane's pessimistic attitude was rubbing off on me.

The next day, I got up earlier of course to get ready for work so I would have time to stop by Duane's to give him his clothes. I packed extra clothes just in case I decided to crash at his place. When I arrived at his apartment, I was in a bad mood. I didn't want to be there. I didn't want to fight. And I didn't want him taking his sweet ass time getting ready for work and possibly making me late. Since we had been in a relationship I was late for work several times. I had to tell my boss stupid reasons why I was late and in truth it was only because Duane took forever to do stuff. He didn't care if he was late for his job but I cared that I was late for mine. I excelled in time management and I intended to keep it that way.

I came into the apartment and asked him to help carry in the laundry. He was in a bad mood too. As he was bringing up the first load of clothes, I was letting him know I didn't have much time and couldn't be here long. I told him to hurry up if he wanted a ride to work.

"Don't bitch at me, Denise." he grumbled as he carried a suitcase up the stairs towards me. Then he started screaming that he didn't have money for what he needed since he had let me borrow all of his.

"For what?" I screamed back. "For pot you mean?"

"I can spend my money on whatever I want," Duane yelled. "It's my money."

"Your right it is," I raged. "But you're going to spend it on what I say you can and you're going to do what I say!"

He didn't like that. "For what you want huh?!" he stomped his feet and punched the fridge a few times. I could understand his anger. I wasn't his boss. I wasn't in charge of his life. When I said that statement, I meant he needed to be smart with his budget if he wanted to have all the things he was constantly bitching to me for not having.

"Sorry I asked you for money!" I yelled, rushing frantically down the steps. "I will get you some damn money!"

"Why, you got some?" Duane angrily asked, following me.

"Yeah I can get you some," I answered, rushing out. He chased after me but stopped when he saw me get into my car and race out of the driveway. I went to the bank and pulled out sixty dollars, which was what I asked for from the payday loan. I went back to Duane's and threw the money down on the floor.

"Wait a minute!" he yelled. He ran down the stairs and picked up the money before getting into the car with me. He was dressed for work so I drove him there. We argued during the entire drive.

"Sorry I had to ask for money!' I screamed. "Sorry I asked for help. Now I know not to do that again! So don't worry about it."

We sat in the restaurant parking lot for a few minutes. It was snowing pretty hard at the time. It was only a few seconds before the windshield was covered in white.

"Why are you so upset at me Denise?" Duane went on. "I don't have to be to work for a half hour. And you have over an hour before you had to work."

"I'm always waiting on you!" I said. "And here I am again….waiting." I indicated I was waiting for Duane to get out of the car so I could leave. He rolled his eyes at me and got out.

I didn't have a very good day at work. I'm sure Duane didn't either. I sent him a text, apologizing for my behavior. He didn't deserve to be treated like that. He said it was ok. We texted the usual I love you and stuff. He asked me to come over later. Then he said I probably shouldn't. Then he would change his mind again. I didn't want to go over there. My stomach was in knots. I felt like I was going to throw up. Then I got a call from Elijah, Duane's old roommate from the shelter. They still stayed in contact. Elijah was telling me about how Duane was showing him the gun. He said it scared him when Duane cocked it back. He said the look on Duane's face really frightened him. He also asked Elijah how he stayed so happy. Elijah told him he thought about the positive things in his life.

"What's something positive that happened to you recently?" Elijah asked him.

Duane thought for a moment and said he had forgiven his father for everything that happened in the past and that they were finally starting to have a decent relationship.

"See," Elijah smiled. "That's a positive. Now what about your girlfriend? That's a good thing right? I wish I had somebody."

"She's always bitching at me." Duane sneered. "I even get bitched at when I'm trying to sleep."

I know Elijah was telling me all this because he was trying to see how I would react. Rumors were still spreading about Duane and I. Elijah was hinting to get some information but I kept quiet. Nonetheless, Elijah was concerned about Duane. I told him I would give Duane a call and see if I could help.

"Are you thinking of harming yourself?" I asked Duane over the phone a little while after I hung up with Elijah. "You wouldn't ever do that would you?"

"No," Duane mumbled.

"You can talk to me about anything," I told him.

"I know." Duane sounded so down, even worse than usual.

"Someone told me that you think I'm a bitch." I sadly informed him. "Do you really think I'm that bad?"

"Who was that?" he asked, offended.

"I'm not going to tell on them." I said.

He was quiet for a moment then said, "I think I know. It had to be Elijah. He was the only person I spoke to since I saw you. And you would've said something earlier." I started to admit it but he cut me off.

"And I didn't say you were a bitch." Duane continued. "I said I even get bitched at for sleeping."

"It's not because you're sleeping." I said as I rolled my eyes. I already had this conversation with him several times in the past. "It's because you're snoring so loud in my ear and I can't sleep."

I apologized again for fighting. I told him I loved him. He kept talking about getting some pot. He wanted me to call my friend George and ask if he could help him out. I told him I was too busy, which I was. Here I am at work trying to make a living. He was just chilling at his house. Why couldn't he call George? He hung out with him a few times before. George gave him weed in the past. I knew George wouldn't think it was odd if Duane called him up.

Duane was getting irritated and saying I wouldn't help him. That was making me upset again. I was trying to work. I couldn't be making drug deals on the shelter's phone. Even if George said yes, we wouldn't be able to get over there until about one in the morning and I had to work the next day. George lived in Mio and it took at least forty minutes to drive there from my house. Once again I was getting upset that I had to constantly drive Duane around. I know he wanted his pot but that wasn't a good reason for me to stay up late and put more miles on the car. I was having a difficult time keeping up on the repairs. Getting the car fixed was what put me in debt in the first place. That's why I had to keep asking for more money from the payday loan. That was why I needed Duane to loan me his entire disability check. That was another reason he was upset. He felt like he wasn't going to survive. I told him to give me a week and I would give most of it back. That wasn't good enough though. He kept worrying and he wouldn't stop!

"Maybe you shouldn't come over tonight," Duane mumbled. He was often in a depressed mood but he was worse tonight. I didn't want to come over if he was angry. I told him that several times. He still sent me a text asking if I'd like to stop by. I didn't want to. But I still didn't want to abandon him. Maybe I would stay for a little bit. Then I would leave after he passed out. I reluctantly went over there.

Chapter 12

Every day is the Same

Minutes before I pulled in the driveway, I received a text from him saying he was going to take a nap but would leave the door unlocked for me. When I arrived at his apartment, I went up the stairs and the only light on was the overhead oven light. I could hear Duane quietly snoring in the bedroom. He didn't wake up when I got there. I was hungry so I made myself a sandwich. I prepared it in the microwave and ate in the living room since the only place he had to sit at was a small card table with a matching fold up chair. By the time I was done eating, he still had not woke up. I decided to take a shower. I was in there for a few minutes.

I don't want to be here, I repeated in my head.

I got out of the shower and put on pajamas. As I was brushing my teeth, I could hear the floor creaking. I felt the presence of someone outside the door. I figured Duane was listening to me. He often did that at my house. I never knew what he was looking for or listening to. I thought it was cute at first but then it just became strange. Spying on me outside the door was too much. I opened it up and he wasn't there, but I know that he had been there. He was still lying in bed but he was no longer sleeping. He was just lying there. I sat down on the floor a few feet away, looking at stuff online with my phone while he talked in a sullen monotone about the same stuff he talked about every day.

"This isn't working." was all he said as he threw the blankets off of him. What wasn't working? Us? His job? Life? I asked him what he was talking about but he didn't answer me. I was getting the feeling that he didn't want me there and that was a huge reason why I didn't want to come over in the first place. He still had the mattress pad from the old house lying next to the bed. I started making it so I could lie down.

"You can have the bed." he said as he sat in the corner to light up a cigarette. Even though he said I could have the bed, that wasn't the message I was getting from him. As he smoked a cigarette he solemnly talked about everything negative in his life. First he talked about having an untreatable and deadly disease, meaning the hepatitis C and it was making him depressed.

"The doctor said that would be a symptom." Duane muttered, flicking his cigarette ashes but barely making them into the ashtray.

"Depression is a symptom of the PTSD," I told him. "That could be why." I was trying to steer away from the hepatitis conversation until Duane knew for sure he had it.

"Maybe." he agreed.

I didn't try to comfort him. I didn't sit next to him. I didn't show him any caring or affection. Not because I didn't care but because I was tired of going over the same stuff with him. It's difficult trying to comfort someone every single day about the same issues. I knew he had problems when I started seeing him. I thought I could handle it. Apparently I couldn't. I was done. I couldn't do it anymore. I was about to go crazy myself.

He went on about how he had no money to buy food. I told him I can bring him food from the shelter. He wasn't starving. He did have food. He was just too lazy to put it in the microwave. If the food didn't involve opening the top and eating it right way then he wouldn't bother with it. I also told him it had only been a couple days since he loaned me the money and I would need more time. He talked about how his food stamps stopped. I told him just to call his caseworker and the issue would be resolved. Again, this was something we had already gone over. He talked about how he hated his job and didn't appreciate "punk high schoolers" ordering him around and treating him like shit. He also mentioned that he was having a hard time going to work every day and holding a job.

"I'm on disability for a reason." he said.

Was his illness so severe that he *couldn't* work? If that was the case, why did he go on and on for months about not having a job and he really needed to get one? I was feeling guilty for pushing him to get a job. I only did that because he told me he had lots of jobs and was capable of having one. If he had told me his PTSD was so out of control then I would never have suggested work. I was only going by what he told me. I wasn't in his head. I didn't see the things he saw. I didn't feel the things he felt. I didn't think the thoughts he did. Now I had to feel bad for helping him get a job?

"If you don't like your job or if it's too much for you, then quit. You don't need it anyway. You make enough money to pay for this place" I advised, continuing to post negative statuses online but not specifying what the problem was.

"Why stop now?" Duane asked.

He was so contradicting. I didn't know what to say. I chose to say nothing. Maybe I should have always kept quiet. I obviously didn't know how to talk to people anyway, especially those with mental problems. I really wasn't a good social worker. Duane continued to say that I wouldn't help him get pot. This pissed me off. I told him I was working and I can't be making calls to people about drugs while I was at work. I didn't have time or energy to make a late night stop almost an hour away. I told him we could get it another day when there was more time.

"I can't believe your blaming me for not getting you weed!" I said.

"Did I say that?" he asked.

"You just did!" I reminded him. I was losing my patience. "You just said I wouldn't help you get pot." He didn't say anything to that. He wasn't making any sense. He was quiet for a moment before going on about social workers.

"They are always in my business," Duane muttered. "They are always going to be in my life." He went on about the time at the shelter when third shift counted his pills back in after his overnight Christmas pass and he only had six. Lloyd, the third shift employee, went through his records and he should have had way more Xanax. He brought the attention to Chad who spoke to him about it. Duane lied and said he was grabbing more at medication time when staff wasn't looking. In reality, he was sharing them with me when he was taking meds on my shift.

"Those were my fucking Xanax." Duane quietly vented. "It's none of his business how many I take." With that, he got up and went to the bathroom to take more. When he came back into the bedroom, he lay back down and continued quietly bitching about his life. He wasn't speaking to or about me in a positive way. He was calmly insulting me with every comment out of his mouth. I had enough. I put my phone in my purse and zipped it back up. When he heard that noise, he panicked. He knew I was going to walk out again. This was the third time in a row.

94

"Don't leave," he said trying to block the door.

I started to cry. I pointed to him and then to myself saying, "Duane, I can't do this anymore." I rushed to put my shoes on. I remember thinking that he was always talking about ending it all and if he was going to do it, he was going to do it anyway and I couldn't stop him. I just didn't want to be there when he did it. I was so scared that I was going to hear the gun go off, I ran so fast down the stairs that I almost fell. I made it almost to the car when he rushed out after me.

"Come back in please," he begged.

"No," I resisted." I want to go home."

"Come back in and get something to eat," Duane persisted.

"I already ate," I answered.

"Please stay!" Duane pleaded.

"If you care about me at all you will let me leave!" I shouted.

He moved out of the way so I could get in the car. "If you cared about me you would stay," he shot right back.

"Apparently not," I muttered and got in. I started to drive away. I watched Duane angrily walk back into his house, his fists were clenched and he gave me a dirty look. I rolled my eyes and drove off into the wintery fog. I never saw him again.

He gave me a call about fifteen minutes later.

"I'd ask you to turn around and come back but I know you're not going to," he muttered. I could tell he was hoping I would do the opposite.

"Yep," I agreed without hesitation. "You're right. I'm not."

"Why are you being so cold towards me?" he said, his voice starting to rise again.

"Because!" I rapidly explained. "You know what Duane, I love you but I'm done."

"*ARE YOU BREAKING UP WITH ME?!*" he screamed.

"Yes I am." I proudly stated. It was time. I couldn't go on with this unhealthy relationship anymore. I couldn't be his therapist or his savior. I couldn't be the person he wanted or needed me to be.

"*Don't do it!*" he warned in a voice I had never heard come out of him before. Then I heard the buttons beep a few times really fast as if he was dialing another phone number.

"Why Duane?" I mocked. "What are you going to do?"

Are you going to kill yourself? I thought. I waited for the threat that I had heard so many times from him before. Silence.

"Duane?" I said. "Duane can you hear me?"

I looked at the phone and the timer was still going which meant the call was still connected. He hadn't hung up. But he wasn't saying anything. Was he even on the phone anymore? I repeated his name a few more times then hung up. I wasn't going to play games with him anymore or waste my time. He often sat on the other end of the phone and I had to call out his name a couple times to get him to answer. It was as if his mind went elsewhere and I had to bring him back to reality. I wasn't the only one he did this to. He wasn't going to do it to me again either.

I felt a sense of relief after I hung up. I felt free. I wanted to be with Duane so much but there was no way we could ever be a healthy and happy couple and live a normal life. I felt as if he was a weight on my shoulder that I was finally strong enough to remove. I drove all the way home and never heard from him again. I was waiting for him to call back and say he was sorry. Then I would say that I was sorry too. Then we would have amazing sex and go back to our vicious cycle of fighting.

A phone call never came.

Chapter 13

The end is creeping in

An hour later I tried to call Duane. The phone rang a couple times then went to voicemail. I left him a voicemail saying, *"I'm sorry for fighting. Let's talk tomorrow when we are not angry anymore."*

I sent him a text message that said the same thing. I figured he would call right back like he usually did. But no call came. Neither did any texts. It was a long night. I didn't sleep well. I took a couple Xanax and fell asleep for a while and would wake back up. Each time I woke up I texted and called Duane. Nothing. Did he break the phone when I told him it was over? I was trying to figure out why the phone made beeping noises.

What if he threw the phone and it broke? Or maybe he passed out from his Xanax? The thought of him shooting himself never really came to my mind. I knew he was scared of death. I didn't think he would ever have the guts to actually take his own life. I thought it was a guilt trip to make me stay. I figured he would down all his pills before he would put a gun to his head. Then I thought maybe he was so mad at me he needed time to be alone. My mind kept racing as I kept trying to call with no success.

A little after three in the morning, I woke up to the sound of my front door slamming and someone walking quickly down the hall to my bedroom. I sensed anger. Then I thought it might be Duane and he got a cab with the money I gave him earlier that day. He had done it before.

"Duane?" I shouted sitting up in bed. I got up to meet him in the hallway but there was nobody there. I went out the living room and nobody was there. The front door was still shut and locked. What the hell? I thought. I wasn't dreaming. I wasn't drunk or high. I know what I heard. Since I lived in a trailer, it wasn't sturdy like a house was. When someone walked around you could feel it wherever you were in the trailer. I heard and felt the floor creaking as if someone were there. I heard the door open. I heard the door close. Yet I was completely alone. My heart began to race and my breathing was shaky. I was starting to worry even more.

I called Duane again and no answer. Then I thought about him shooting himself. I called the Gaylord police asking if gunshots had been reported. They said no yet I could tell they thought this was a weird question. I felt relieved. If Duane had used the gun, the tenants in the other apartments would have heard it. Then I'm sure they would've called it in. Duane was scheduled to work at seven in the morning. I would call him again a little before then when he would for sure be up and getting ready for work. I fell asleep for a while longer.

I woke up again shortly after six in the morning. I checked my phone. No missed calls or texts from anyone. I called Duane again. He had to be up by now getting ready for work. No answer. I texted him saying if he didn't answer me I would be sending a cop over there to check on him I figured this would get him to respond. He hated anyone coming over unannounced, especially the cops. But he never responded. That was when I really started to panic.

Around seven, I called his work asking if he had shown up yet. They said no but it wasn't unusual for him to be a few minutes late. I asked them how he was acting the day before. The woman I was speaking to had not worked with him so she couldn't answer my question. I asked her to have him call me when he got there to make sure he was ok. I also told her I had a feeling he may have harmed himself or was in trouble. Another hour went by and Duane never called me. This told me that he didn't go to work. However I wasn't ready to believe he was dead. The way he was talking about hating his job could explain why he didn't show up to work. I think he wanted to quit. I called the police and explained to them that he didn't show up for work and he wasn't answering is phone. The cop said he was an adult and wasn't considered missing yet but he would go over and see if he was alright.

I went about my day as usual. I cleaned my house, ran errands, and got ready for work. Periodically I would try Duane's cell phone again. Now it would just go straight to voicemail. I called his landlord and asked her to check on him. She was out of town so she couldn't go over there. She let me know that her and some clients that were downstairs in the salon heard the fight between us. She said it was very disturbing and she called the police. They must have showed up after I took him to work. She was upset and asked for it to not happen again.

"I'm trying to run a business," she explained. "And I can't do that when there is screaming and banging going on in the apartment above it." I apologized, advised it wouldn't happen again, and hung up the phone.

The cop also went over to the apartment and knocked loudly for a several minutes before leaving. I decided to go over there myself and see if he would let me in. When I got to his apartment, nothing looked unusual. It was very quiet but that was typical. I peered into the window so I can see up the stairs. Duane's shoes were at the top of the steps still in the exact same spot. So if he had gone anywhere he didn't use those shoes. There were no footprints going in or out of the home so that told me if he was up there, he hadn't come out. I could also faintly see the oven light still on. This I did find strange because Duane only used that light when he was using the stove. If he were in there right now using it, I would have seen a shadow moving around. I know if he heard me knocking he would have looked to see who it was, especially when I texted him a while ago saying I was on my way over. As usual, I still had no answers. I went to work and tried to focus. Once in a while I tried to call Duane. Still nothing.

A little later in the evening, a couple by the name of Crysten and Roy came in to chart. They were a nice couple from Georgia who were trying to get custody of their children. They were advised to come to the shelter and go through our program so they could find permanent stable housing to bring their two young kids home. I liked them. They were trustworthy, respectful, and followed the rules as best as they could. I knew that Duane had befriended them as well as they had visited him a few times in his apartment. When they came in the office, I asked them if they had talked to Duane. They didn't look surprise that I was asking about Duane. However, they seemed surprised that I would be asking them.

"You guys are friends with him right?" I asked even though I knew the answer. Pretending not to know things was something I was getting very good at.

"Yes," Crysten said. "But we haven't talked to him in a couple days. We texted a few times but no texts back."

"Nobody has heard from him I guess." I went on. "He was very upset the other day and he didn't report to work."

Crysten looked at me intensely and said, "Maybe he had a fight with his girlfriend."

"Maybe," I quickly said. "From what I hear she can be a huge bitch."

"Do you know his girlfriend?" they both wondered.

I didn't say anything but tried to look puzzled the best that I could.

"Are you his girlfriend?" Crysten smiled. Still I said nothing. My silence told them what they wanted to know.

"Please don't tell anyone." I asked kindly. "I could lose my job."

This was the first time I actually admitted that Duane and I were a couple. I was scared to let it out but at the same time I was relieved to finally tell someone. I trusted Crysten and Roy. Something about them told me they wouldn't repeat a word.

"Yeah we could tell," they said. "We could see the way y'all acted when you were around each other or someone was talking about y'all."

"Do you think anyone else noticed?" I wondered.

"I don't think so." Roy said.

"Besides," Crysten went on. "It's none of their business."

I smiled weakly and continued to tell them about me and Duane's last conversation. I said I called the police and have been trying to get ahold of him. I told them he had a gun and I was worried he harmed himself. It wasn't like him to ignore me this long. I asked them if they would go over to his apartment and see if they could possibly get him to answer them. They said sure and left.

It wasn't long before they called and said they knocked very loudly for at least five minutes and nothing. They said lights were on but no movement. They tried to get in, as did I, but it was dead bolted from inside. I thanked them for trying. I would try again after work. I called the police again and told them the same story. I explained that nobody had heard from Duane and that was not normal. The police man said they would go over there again. About an hour later he called me back. He said there was no answer. However, there were footprints going up the stairs.

"That's because I just had my friends go over there," I told him.

"No." he explained. "I meant the steps inside the house. There was snow on them as if someone had been outside and then went back inside."

I thanked him and felt a sense of relief. This proved that either Duane or someone else had been in the home recently. Maybe he had left to go get cigarettes. Or perhaps the knocking woke him up and he went to see who it was. Crysten and Roy said nothing about snow being in the steps while they were there. I still planned to go over there after work. I prayed that Duane was ok and wanted to finally see him. I missed him so much and wanted to give him the tightest hug. When I got out of work I went straight over to the apartment. The snow on the steps had melted.

However, there were steps going out to the road. Someone had been here recently. The door was still bolted. All the same lights were still on. I noticed the bathroom light was on as it was the night before. Duane was very finicky about turning lights off when he wasn't using a room. The chance of him using the bathroom every time I was there was very thin. I knew something was wrong. I knew he was up there and he wasn't ok. I drove to the police station to file a report. The clerk told me I had to see the city police because of where in Gaylord the incident was happening. I drove over there and repeated my story a millionth time. Two police officers said they would go over there and call me when they found out something. I drove home and cried, leaving a message on Duane's phone. I said *"I was sorry for being mean to you"* and *"What did you do?"* and *"Please be ok."*

Chapter 14

The night all the butterflies died

I pulled into my driveway at 12:25 am and I had a missed call. It was the police. I called them back and that was when I had to start answering all the questions about Duane's family. This was when they told me they had to break the door down and found him dead. They couldn't tell me anything else since I wasn't family. I ran into my house and downed the sedatives and sobbed for what seemed like hours. My friend Valerie told me to come over and stay the night. When I got there I could tell she had been drinking and crying. She held me tight for several minutes and told me she was sorry over and over. She talked about last Christmas, when I had brought Duane and Evan over there for dinner. Valerie told me about when she asked Duane if he was going to see his family for the holidays.

"Christmas is just another day for me." he admitted to her. "My family doesn't call or visit. It's always been that way for me."

This made Valerie cry.

"How can someone not see their family at Christmas?' she cried. She felt so bad for him when she heard that. She did her best to console me and tell me that breaking up with him was just a small part of a bigger part of his problems. Duane taking his life was not about me. Sure it hurt when I said it was over, and that may have been the last straw for him, but he was already gone way before then.

This is not your fault they all kept saying.

I tried hard to believe it. Questions kept entering my mind though. What if I hadn't broken up with him? What if I hadn't borrowed money and then he felt like he couldn't pay for anything? What if I had stayed instead of running out the door? What if I held him more? Then I thought about all the times I had an opportunity to get rid of the gun. It had always made me nervous. I was scared of what he would do if I got rid of it. What if I had sold it? What if I threw it in the lake? What if I had just dropped it off at the police station and drove away? What if I had only hid the magazine clip or the bullets? All these scenarios ran through my mind. That was why I felt guilty. That was why I felt I was to blame. I was the closest person to him at that point in his life.

The gun was kept at my house for quite a while and I could have done something then. Why didn't I get rid of it when he mentioned it every time we had a fight? How could I not see what he was feeling, planning, or thinking? That stupid fucking gun! If it wasn't here, Duane would still be here. Then I thought about how unhappy he was and how much I could see now that he wanted to die. Who am I to make him stay? It really hurt that he took his life. It also hurt to think that he was suffering here in our world if I hadn't gotten rid of the gun. I wasn't sure what was worse. Losing a loved one to suicide or seeing a loved one suffer? Sometimes I think it was the best thing for him and all of us. At least he wasn't in pain anymore. He was a burden. He couldn't get it together and we all suffered trying to help him all the time.

I left Valerie's house shortly after five in the morning. I was fine for the first few seconds after I woke up until I remembered Duane was dead. Then the sad reality set in once again. Duane was dead and I would never see or hear from him again. I went back home and attempted to sleep awhile. I woke up again at 8:23 in the morning. I will never forget that time. I put on some songs that Duane and I enjoyed listening to together and I just cried. I was confused about how to handle this. I couldn't concentrate on anything else. I also couldn't just sit there and think about it all day. It was as if I was being pulled in different directions on how to deal with this. At the same time, I was frozen in one spot because I didn't know which direction to take. I kept saying I was sorry. I felt so guilty. I kept going over the last couple weeks in my mind and thought about how things that could have been different. I wished I had not been so mean to him. If he were going to leave this earth I wished our last moments together would have been loving. Now I was stuck with the memory of us fighting and me saying I didn't care about him. It wasn't true. I did care about him. I did love him.

"I think I love you more than you love me," Duane mumbled a couple weeks prior when all the fighting has started to get worse.

I was stuck with all those negative memories and reactions. I was so mad and I had to live with that for the rest of my life. I thought about it all the time. Now I understand when people say always tell those close to you that you love them. You never know when that will be your last opportunity to say so. Even if we were not meant to be together, I would've always wanted to know how he was and be there for him. Now there I was in my cold, lonely trailer. For the first time in my life I was completely alone. I had always had friends, family, or a boyfriend living with me. Evan wasn't even there for me to care for. I was completely alone and it was creepy. I felt like Duane was still there and that made things even weirder. I continued to cry as I listened to music.

I realized I had to keep busy. It was the weekend and I didn't have to work. Duane and I were planning to spend the weekend together and now that wasn't a possibility. I cleaned the house and started getting rid of anything Duane had left there. He wasn't going to need them anymore. Holding on to his possessions was only hurting and making me cry more. Valerie texted me awhile later asking how I was doing. I told her I was scared to be alone. She told me to come over. A couple other friends had texted me saying they were going out later. I wasn't feeling up to hanging out but I also knew it would help keep my mind busy. Plus, I had not seen any of them in months so it would be great catching up.

I went over to Valerie's and had some coffee while chatting with her and her parents. She suggested I go out. I needed to let loose and have fun. I asked her if she wanted to go but she wasn't feeling up to it. Before I left her house, I called the police station to see if they had gotten ahold of anyone in Duane's family. I had stuff in his apartment that I needed back so it was very important that I spoke with someone soon. The police had told me that they had spoken with Duane's father. That was where I admitted to the cop that Duane and I were more than friends and that our relationship was rocky because of his PTSD. He was unable to give me any information on Duane but did give me his dad's number. I told Valerie I needed to make the call and be completely alone to do so. I knew it would be very emotional for me so I headed back to my empty home.

I pulled into my driveway and took a Xanax before calling Duane's father, whose name was also Duane. I was so nervous. I had never spoken to him before and I was scared of how he was going to react to me. I felt like he was going to blame me for what happened. After a couple of rings, a deep voice said, "Hello?"

He sounded just like Duane, with the New York accent. If I had not known any better, I would think I was talking to Duane. It took all the power I had not to lose it over the phone.

"May I speak to Duane please?" I nervously asked.

"This is Duane," he said.

"Hi Duane," I went on. "My name is Denise. I was dating your son Duane."

After a couple seconds, he put two and two together. "Oh hi Denise," he said. He was actually pleasant. Duane had always described his dad as overbearing and argumentative. He said his dad was always debating with him on every topic they spoke about. Yet he seemed quite the opposite.

"What happened?" I asked up front.

"Well," Duane answered, "Maybe you can help me put the pieces together. And then I can do the same for you."

Mr. Cambell went on to explain the police had come over to his mother's house, who was Duane's grandmother. They woke her at about two in the morning to give her the news. Duane had her as an emergency contact. Duane had spoken highly of his grandmother. He said she was one of the few people in his life that made him feel loved and that he had fond memories of her. Mr. Cambell continued to say that Duane had shot himself. He was angry that someone with a suicidal past could obtain a gun. Duane told me he had bought it from a local sporting goods store. The truth was the gun was illegally bought from someone Duane knew. It was not registered.

I learned that "the crazy person" who stabbed Duane in the arm years ago was Duane himself. When he did that, he was put into intensive care for a month. The doctors had to take a skin graft from his thigh and applied it to his arm so

109

the skin would grow back. When this happened, they ruled it as a suicide attempt. In many states, those who attempt suicide cannot own a firearm. This was why Duane had to buy it illegally. I knew Duane was depressed but I had no idea it was this bad. The more Mr. Cambell talked about his son, the more I realized I didn't know much about him. I remember Duane telling me he had things to say but was afraid of how I would react. He always thought I would leave just like all the others did before. His father talked about how Duane was the happiest baby. He was always laughing. Then at the age of two, his mother Hilary kidnapped him and didn't let Duane see him for two years. When he finally did see him, he said his eyes looked "dead" and he was all "screwed up". He asked Hilary what happened but it only turned into arguments.

From what both Duane and his father told me, Hilary was an addict for a long time and she brought her son to weird places when she got drugs. She hung around strange people who she let molest Duane because she was so high. Duane said she knew about it and didn't do anything to stop it. Mr. Cambell said he heard that story before but thought it was too low even for Hilary. I learned that Duane would sometimes wait several hours for his mother to pick him up and she wouldn't show. If she did, she would call Mr. Cambell an hour later screaming that she was going to bring Duane back because she couldn't handle him. Duane struggled in school. As he got older, things just got worse. He didn't have many friends. He was always getting in fights. He was kicked out of school. He couldn't hold a job. He would get girlfriends but they never lasted long. He could never get it together.

When Duane turned 18, he moved to the Detroit area to be close to his mother but it never worked out. He wanted to have a close relationship with her but it was never possible. He would try over and over to reinvent his life and it never lasted long. At one point, he went out to California for a year then came back. He was even worse by then. He never told anyone why he went out there or what he did. That part of his life was and always will be a mystery. When Duane was 25, his younger brother had committed suicide. He was found hanging in a closet. He was only sixteen years old. Around that time, Duane's girlfriend Kelly had broken up with him as well. This happened on New Year's Eve. While Duane was eating steak, she told him it was over. That was when he stabbed himself in the arm. He told me it was one quick stab. According to his family, he stabbed himself several times. That was why the doctors took a while to repair it. He had severely damaged the veins there and they had to be extremely careful when removing the blade.

When telling me his story a couple months prior, Duane admitted he had a breakdown and it was understandable. He had just lost his brother and was losing a woman he dated for a while whom he was in love with. I don't think he ever got over her. She visited him once the entire month he was in the hospital. Then he never saw her again. A few months later, he emailed her to say he was sorry that he put her through witnessing him stab himself. But she never responded. Maybe that was why he couldn't move on from her. He needed closure and he never got it. It was apparent in his dreams. Some nights I would hear him talking in his sleep. He always sounded angry and he was swearing at someone to get away from him. Then we would talk about a woman named Kelly. When I asked him about it, he rolled his eyes and got irritated with me.

Then he met Amber. She was his longest relationship yet was also a lot younger than him. I think she stuck with him for three years because she was young and didn't know any better. Duane had gotten close to Amber and her family but they too had a rocky relationship. Awhile after they broke up, Duane tried hard to keep her in his life, almost to the point of being obsessed. Her family was still helping out long after they called it quits. He had gotten an apartment that he stayed in for a while. It was there that Amber brought her new boyfriend over, to which Duane said the only reason he could think of was to get him angry. It worked. Duane got into a physical fight with Amber's new boyfriend a few times. This left the man feeling threatened so he got a restraining order against Duane. Duane insisted he wasn't a threat. He was only defending himself. Yes he was jealous that Amber left him for this guy, but it wasn't the reason he despised him so much. It turned out this new boyfriend was very abusive to Amber and this angered Duane. She went to the hospital a few times because of her injuries.

"Next time he's gonna end up killing her," he once told me.

Duane's landlord was upset by the fighting but chose to let him continue to rent the apartment. Then one night Duane's neighbors were downstairs smoking crack and being extremely loud. Instead of calling the landlord, Duane chose to handle the situation himself. Nobody is sure what exactly happened that night. However, according to Mr. Cambell, whatever Duane said or did scared the entire building so much that he was the one who was kicked out, not the people partying. Duane's father also told me about some people that Duane's half-brother, Steve, knew who let Duane rent a room from them. He didn't stay there long either. Apparently, Duane would listen to music really loud in his room all the time. He put strange posters on the walls and door of his room. The scariest thing he did was play with his gun. This freaked the roommates out so they told Duane to leave.

Shortly after that, Duane rented a room from an older woman whose boyfriend set her on fire a little while after he moved in. She was burned pretty badly as was the house. Duane had to leave there too. He said she survived the ordeal and ended up going back to the man who tried to kill her. Duane moved around a lot. It was his anger and his behavior that ruined things for him. I could see why people would be scared of him. I was scared of him when we first met. But he was anything but scary. Yes, he had a mean side. But his mean side wasn't to hurt others. It was his way of venting all the hurt that he had been through. He also had a loving and caring side that I was so blessed to get to know. He was a scared and hurt guy trying to find someone to love him. All of him. Not just the good parts. He wanted someone to love even the most diseased parts of his mind, body, and soul.

"He has been through so much shit!" Mr. Cambell screamed over the phone. From being molested at age four and not having a mother who wanted him and so he had to move around, it made sense that he was angry all the time and his relationships suffered. He had a lot of negative emotions built up that he never knew how to handle in a healthy way. Mr. Cambell felt that his son was freaked out about having hepatitis and that was the boiling point for him. Learning about Duane's past only raised more questions instead of answering the ones I already had. Duane was even more mysterious than ever.

Chapter 15

Something for the pain

I tried to push all the depressing thoughts away and get ready to go out with my friends. It was a decent night. It was good catching up with them. I had a good time, but every so often I would remember that Duane was dead and it was my fault. I kept getting drinks but they didn't really have an effect on me. I missed Duane so much already. He was the only person I had ever met where just simply hanging out was fun. I was never bored with him. He may have been depressed, hostile, and tormented. He was a lot of things, both positive and negative. Whatever Duane was, I know one thing he was not; boring. I found him exciting and interesting. The darkness that surrounded him was what I was attracted to the most. Even in the end where it caused us to fight and possibly start hating each other, it was the mystery about him that intrigued me.

The rest of the weekend was a blur. I tried to keep busy but give myself time to grieve. I received a call from Margaret, Duane's grandmother. She was the one he referred to as *Nana* and who was biggest inspiration of his life. She thanked me for caring a lot about her grandson. She didn't want to think about how long his body would have been in that apartment if I had not been so persistent with the police. She asked me if I had any pictures. I told her I just had a few from my phone. I said I would go through them and send her everything I had.

Later that evening I got a call from Hilary. She started crying when she asked me, "Did Duane ever tell you that he hated me?"

"No." I told her. "He didn't hate you. He just...." I wasn't sure how to say it without making her feel even worse than she already did. "He sometimes blamed you for the way that he was."

I knew Duane had issues because of her. We all knew it. She was a big reason he was hurting all the time. However, I didn't think it was right to blame her or anyone. People can't help what happens to them. But they do have control over how they handle it. Duane never handled it, which was what ate at him every day. Hilary told me similar things about her son that Mr. Cambell said. She said he was never able to get it together. He would do ok for a little while. Then something would piss him of and his actions would ruin everything. She also asked me for pictures. She hadn't physically seen her son since he was 18. That was twelve years ago. They spoke on the phone, but it would either be them arguing about the past or Duane leaving really goofy message on her voicemail. A lot of the messages were him singing songs in weird voices or just rambling on about nothing. Hilary thought it was strange but now she misses getting those messages.

The next night I received a phone call from Duane's brother Steve, who lived in Tennessee. This was the brother that was leaving Duane very violent messages on his phone about kicking his ass. Those were the messages Duane asked me to listen to the first time he came to chart with me at the shelter. I advised him to stop listening and just delete them. Steve told me about the messages. I told him I listened to them all. He said he was leaving them because Duane would leave them too or send threatening texts.

When he would call Duane back, he never got an answer and that was why he left those messages. He agreed that him and Duane butted heads a lot. He said it was because it was hard to talk to Duane, which I knew it was. Everyone had to watch what they said without him getting upset or taking it the wrong way. Steve told me about how he let Duane come stay with him and his father but that only lasted a week. Duane had originally agreed to work and pay the bills while he stayed there. Yet when Duane arrived in Tennessee he didn't try to find a job. He ate all their food and didn't contribute. Steve said that was the complete opposite of what Duane said it would be like.

Once Steve realized it was going to be the same like all the other times before, he told Duane he had to leave. There was a shelter nearby called *New Hope*. However, the only way someone could get in was to say they had a drug or alcohol addiction. Duane did not have an addiction but Steve said to lie and act like he did. Whatever Duane told the employees there worked because he got in. However, as usual, he was forced to leave a short time later. Steve said when he went to pick him up from the shelter, Duane was sitting next to a garbage can looking rough and dirty, smoking cigarette butts that he found on the ground.

"It looked so bad Denise," Steve told me. "Duane looked like a homeless person. He looked like he had been homeless for a long time."

That following Monday morning, I received a text from Crysten, warning me that Chad found out about Duane. She said I should be prepared for questions. I was really nervous about talking to Chad. He was very good at reading people. I could lie to him and he would still know the truth. I didn't want to go to work anyway. I was very sad and I couldn't hide it. The clients would all know what happened and question me. Or question each other and start more rumors. People knew Duane and I were involved. They didn't know the exact facts, but knew something was there. Duane and I were a hot topic for months now. The suicide was just more fuel to the fire. When I got to work, Chad asked me if I heard the bad news.

"Yes" I mumbled as I clocked in for my shift.

Chad gave an uneasy laugh. "Good." he said. "I really didn't want to be the one to tell you." Instead of leaving like he usually would, he sat at the desk and scrolled through social media and online game stats. He was trying to get me to open up about Duane. I told him about the last time I saw him, but I left out certain parts. I didn't want to indicate that there was a relationship, although Chad already knew there was something.

"I know things," he muttered to me while I was telling my story. I ignored the comment and went on. I told Chad about how Duane was worried he would give people hepatitis and how he hated the fact that most of his bosses were still in high school.

"I can understand that," Chad said. "It would be difficult having someone a lot younger than me telling me what to do every day. I can understand it made him feel inferior."

I didn't tell him about how Duane had mentioned Chad needed to mind his own business about the Xanax. I'm not sure what I told him that day but I guarantee I implicated myself. I know I mentioned that Duane and I had the same taste in music. Looking back, I'm not sure why I told him that. It had to indicate something personal between us. I told him I let Duane borrow some of my furniture and I needed it back. I couldn't find my glasses either and I had a feeling they were in the apartment too. Chad was letting me vent but I also knew he was trying to be nosy. My story had gaps in it and I'm sure he sensed that.

After he left, I tried to stay busy by doing my normal duties. Occasionally clients would need assistance and look at me as though they were waiting for me to cry or say something about Duane. I stayed strong. It is never a good idea to let your personal business get in the way of work. I had already let that happen and look where it gotten me. I would have expected to lose my job or perhaps Duane cheated on me or even hit me. I never would have expected this of all things to happen. I tried to focus on anything other than Duane. It was difficult. I kept going over scenarios in my head. I felt like he was dead because of me. I could have prevented this. How stupid and blind was I to not see the warning signs?

Elijah called the office later and told me how he had found out Duane took his life. He said he was walking by the apartment and saw a white ServPro van in the driveway. Servpro is a restoration company who has exceptional cleaning service. Their motto is *"Like it never happened."* They dealt with intense cases such as flooding and of course death. Elijah said there must be a mess in the apartment for them to come in. He said he went into the salon below and spoke to Janice.

"Is he dead?" he asked bluntly. "Yes." she said quickly yet sadly.

"What happened?" he continued, although Elijah was sure he already knew.

"He shot himself." Janice replied.

"When?" Elijah pressed.

"He was found yesterday," Janice explained, "But the police said he was dead for a couple days."

Elijah's story chilled me. Duane was very important to both of us. Elijah and I also built a friendship while he was at the shelter and even afterwards. Elijah was a recovering heroin addict and he had managed to stay sober for months now. I was concerned if Duane's death was going to cause him to relapse. He was a good person and I was proud that he was able to change his life around. He spoke at AA/NA meetings weekly and told his story to people who were trying to kick their addiction habits. Elijah felt like he could have stopped the suicide as well, since Duane had showed him the gun a week earlier. The look on Duane's face when he cocked the trigger back scared Elijah and it bothered him ever since. He felt that he had the opportunity to take the gun when Duane was unaware. We could all repeat the events over and over in our heads. The way I saw it was if it wasn't meant to be, it wouldn't have happened. I believe that everything happens the way it is supposed to. If Duane were meant to live then he would have. If we were meant to take the gun and get rid of it then we would have.

Chapter 16

Nutshell

Work wasn't as hard as though it would be. It was the half hour drive home that got me. It was going home to a cold and empty house that was unbearable. I cried most of the time thinking about how mean I was to Duane that night. I took Xanax as soon as I got home. I curled up in a ball on the couch. I kept the television on for noise most of the time. It was too quiet in the trailer. The television helped me feel less lonely.

I tried to eat here and there but everything literally felt and tasted like cardboard in my mouth. I forced myself to drink some milk and juice. I drank just enough to put something in my stomach to stop it from growling. It took every effort I had just to drink a cup of it. My sleep was fragmented. I was exhausted yet my heart wouldn't stop racing and relax enough to sleep. If it weren't for the Xanax I don't think I would have slept at all. Sometimes I took two and they had little effect. I felt awful mentally and physically. I wanted to die. I didn't deserve to live. Someone who treats a person so badly and would just let them die is the one who should be dead. I should be in Duane's place. All he wanted was someone to love and care about him and I abandoned him and made him feel more unwanted than he already did. After a thousand negative thoughts went through my mind, I finally drifted off to sleep. I was out long enough just to wake a couple hours later to cry some more. Then I would fall asleep again and repeat the process.

The next morning I called Duane's landlord. She told me the police found him sitting in a chair. I could tell she felt freaked out by the whole situation, and who could blame her? Not only is it a terrible tragedy to find someone dead in your apartment, but someone who just moved in two weeks prior and then shot themselves? Now she had to deal with the aftermath. She had to clean it up, and possibly do remodeling to fix whatever damage was done.

"Did you go up there?" I asked.

"I chose not to." she answered.

"So you're not sure what's up there?" I wondered.

Janice said the only time she had been up there was when she showed Duane and Rosie the apartment. She had no idea what all he moved in with. She was too spooked to go upstairs while his stuff was still in there. She had no idea on the condition his belongings.

"The police said there was minimal damage." she explained. "But they had to cut up some of the carpet because of the hepatitis C."

She asked me about his family and if anyone could get his stuff. I told her they were all out of state and requested I go in there, which was true. Mr. Cambell didn't want to fly out for just some clothes and papers. He asked me what all was in the storage unit downstate. I told him there were a lot of things in there but I wasn't sure what they were. He said he had been paying the storage bill for over two years but he had never been there nor knew what was stored inside. He was not thrilled about flying in from Pennsylvania if whatever was in there didn't have a lot of value. Duane told me his car was full of stuff too but it was locked up in

Amber's driveway.. Duane had all the keys to everything in the apartment.

I asked Janice if I could go into the apartment and get Duane's belongings and return them to his family. She said that would be fine. I sent Crysten and Roy a message asking if they would accompany me. I couldn't do it alone. They said yes. We planned to be there the next day around noon, which would give me a couple hours before work. When I arrived at Duane's apartment, Crysten and Roy were already there waiting for me. I had taken a Xanax before I left the house but as soon as I got into the driveway, my heart began to race and my hands shook. This was going to be so hard for me. I took another one to calm my nerves. Crysten and Roy said they had already let the landlord know they were there and they were just waiting for me. It had only been a couple seconds from my arrival that Janice's boyfriend came around the corner to unlock the apartment. Janice was busy with a customer so she couldn't come out herself.

As Janice's boyfriend unlocked the door, I felt Crysten rub my back to give me strength. She had been through a similar situation in her life. She told me this would be the hardest part, going to the place where "it" happened. In Crysten's situation, she had broken up with her boyfriend too, but he left a suicide note saying he did it because of her. Then she had to go identify his body. With her going through such a terrible ordeal, I confided in her about Duane. I listened to her when she gave me advice on how to get through it. As we walked up the stairs to Duane's apartment, everything looked the same from the last time I was there. I could feel the sadness in the air. There was tension and anger. It was if Duane was still in there watching us.

"Take as long as you need to," Janice's boyfriend told us and he walked back downstairs to the salon.

I began grabbing all of my belongings such as my glasses and personal hygiene products. The bathroom was the same as I had left it, which indicated Duane never used it after me. I took the radio out of there. Duane liked to listen to music when he was in the shower, a habit which I had adapted from being with him. I was curious what he had last listened to so I peeked inside the radio. It was a Fiona Apple CD. I grabbed the coffee pot that I just given to him for Christmas three weeks earlier. I didn't take many clothes. Just the ones I had bought him recently that he hadn't worn yet. The tags were still on them so I was going to return them. He had a few funny shirts that I like to wear to bed so I grabbed those. They still smelled like him.

I told Crysten and Roy to take anything they needed for their new home they would be moving into soon. They grabbed some dishes and bathroom stuff. Duane had this toy bird that would make sexual comments and shake his feathers so they grabbed that. It was hilarious. We all cracked up anytime it was turned on. They wanted to take his *TOOL* collection but I asked that I keep them. They were very important to him and it helped me stay connected to him.

They took the microwave and all his movies. I grabbed his huge book of CD's and the money on the table that I had thrown at him that day. I grabbed his box of personal papers to send to his father. I saw the restraints in the closet and thought about taking them. I decide not to because he was the only person who had tied me up. I could never use them with someone else. It would remind me of him and be too painful.

123

In the middle of the bedroom floor was where he had taken his life. I could tell because that was where a chunk of the carpet had been cut out from the blood. The chair he had sat in was now folded up in the corner as clean as it was the day it came from the store. If it weren't for the carpet gone, there would be no evidence of what had happened in there. However, you could feel the loneliness and depression all through the apartment. I wanted to hurry and get out of there. The air was tight and I felt like I was suffocating from sadness. I sat on the floor and cried.

"I know you guys told me this wasn't my fault," I mumbled, "But please remind me again."

Crysten sat down in front me and looked me in the eyes. In a comforting voice, she assured me this was not my fault. I couldn't blame or be hard on myself. I had let her read the card he wrote me at Christmas. She told me he had checked out of life long before this and there was nothing I could have done to change things. Taking one last look around, we all decided we had grabbed everything we wanted.

As Roy was putting stuff in the trunk, Janice's boyfriend came back outside and asked where the apartment key as. I showed him all of Duane's set of keys but none of them were to the apartment. We went through Duane's coat pocket but no luck. I told him none of us seen keys lying around. The key was never found. I went into the salon to tell Janice we were done and what was all left upstairs. She gave me a tight hug and told me how sorry she was.

I told Crysten and Roy thank you for being there and headed off to work. When I got there, Meredith wanted to see me in her office. At first I was scared because this was the part where I get fired for being inappropriate with a client. That wasn't what happened though. She knew I was very close to Duane and wanted me to vent to her. I told her the same stuff I told Chad, but I left a lot out. I'm sure she knew more than she let on but she calmly listened to me. Then she told me something I would never forget.

"I don't like to see you hurting, but chances are you're going to be hurt again in your life," Meredith explained. "But I think the reason we get hurt is so we don't forget how to love."

After our meeting, I came out into the office where Chad was. He told me that some of the clients would like to have a memorial service for Duane. It was decided it would happen the following Sunday. I told Chad to do it a couple hours before my shift so I can pull myself together if need be. Meredith began working on a pamphlet to hand out to anyone who chose to attend the service. Some clients said they wanted to cook something for the occasion so we began to come up with a small dinner menu. Work was the same where I pretended I was ok although I wasn't. I focused on my duties yet at the same time I wasn't really paying attention to what was going on around me. I just wanted to make it through so I could get in my car and cry all the way home like I had been doing for days now. It felt like the pain was never going to end.

Chapter 17

Stitches

When I got home that night, I brought in all of Duane's stuff I recovered from the apartment. I was so tired and wanted to sleep but it was creepy having his stuff there. Everything smelled like him and I felt like he was next to me. Even though I loved his scent and wanted him with me, it was eerie and I couldn't package his stuff fast enough. I went through his cd's and took the ones him and I listened to. At first I was going to keep all of them. Yet as I went through the hundreds of albums, I noticed he had a lot of death metal and anti-Christian artists. I was completely against what they stood for.

In the end, I took about twenty discs then shipped the rest to his father. In another box, I put all his personal belongings such as paperwork, his ID, church stuff, books, and anything personal that could tell his father a little bit about the son he never really got to know. Some of the stuff I put in the box was strange. He had a notebook of poems and pictures he had drawn. They didn't make sense and they were somewhat disturbing. I was not sure if I should send that because it may creep out Mr. Cambell and only cause more questions. Yet he needed to see everything so I put it in the box.

I shipped the stuff out the next morning before work. It cost a lot but I knew the family would appreciate it. I had also gone through Duane's phone for any decent pictures to send to his family. I went through my phone as well. Unfortunately, I did not have many. I took the little that I had and printed them out. They were dark and hard to see but they were better than nothing. I made an extra copy of all the pictures for myself. I regret not taking more. Duane and I were so used to hiding our relationship that when we took pictures of ourselves we would delete it as to not leave evidence. A couple days later I received a letter from Margaret. She thanked me for the pictures and told me she hoped I was doing okay. She was a having a difficult time. She knew as the days passed she would have more peace. Duane's father gave me a call the day after that and told me he received both packages. He had only opened the one with all the music. He was confused as to why I sent it since I was originally going to keep it.

"I took what I liked." I told him. "A lot of that music is too heavy for me. Plus, he told me you liked Pink Floyd and artists like that. There's quite a bit of that in there."

I knew Duane's father wasn't going to like most of what was in the book. I mentioned that Steve asked about it. Mr.Cambell was glad to give anyone whatever they wanted of Duane's, but they needed to reach out to him. He wasn't going to call or hunt them down. From the way he spoke of them, he had never met any of them. He just heard the horrible stories about them from his son. Duane often said negative things about everyone especially when he got mad. He didn't have a cruel heart but he was so used to having his feelings hurt that he expected that from everyone he encountered in his life. It was no surprise that he told his father all about the arguments and the bad moments with the family.

"I haven't gone through the other box yet," Mr.Cambell sadly told me. "I'm assuming its more personal stuff right?"

"Yes." I answered.

"I'll look at that later," he mumbled. "I'm not ready yet."

He told me about how there were times Duane hinted to come back home but he highly suggested him not to. Not because he didn't care about his son. It was because the times in the past never worked out and it only caused drama and tension with the other family members. Mr. Cambell now wishes he would have done that. That would be his lifetime regret about this whole situation. I know what ifs were running through his head too. What if Duane had come back to Pennsylvania to start over? Would he still be alive today? Would he have finally gotten his life together? Before hanging up, Duane said he had sent me something in the mail and to watch for it. That was the last time I spoke to him.

A couple days later, I received a card with a gift certificate to a local restaurant as a thank you for sending all Duane's stuff. It was a nice card stating that he was glad Duane had me to spend time with. *I know Duane loved you* the card read. Hilary called me later asking if I sent out any of Duane's things. I told her I sent them to his father since nobody else contacted me sooner. I just wanted the stuff out of my house. I told her I did send copies of the pictures from my phone.

In the meantime, between all the phone calls and sending Duane's stuff out, I attended my first therapy session. I was originally supposed to go to talk about my divorce. However, with Duane's death just days before, I wanted to talk about that instead. My divorce was not something I was focused on. Duane's suicide had devastated me that I too didn't feel like living.

I spent my days trying to look and act normal but I was in a daze. I just existed. I couldn't eat. I couldn't sleep. I didn't want to talk to anyone. I knew I had to keep going because life doesn't stop. Duane chose to end his life. His story ended that day. But mine continued. Just because his story stopped didn't mean mine was going to. I had to go on even though I didn't feel like it. I wanted to die. I missed him so much. I wanted to be where he was. I wanted to say I was sorry and that I loved him.

My therapist told me what I already knew. I was feeling guilty. She said I had nothing to feel guilty about. In time I would realize that. For now, I needed to feel the pain to get through it. She said it was important to eat and drink. She said I experienced trauma and when that happens, it is normal for people to lose their appetites because of the depression. What people forget is when you stop nourishing your body, it slowly shuts down as to protect itself and preserve vitamins and energy.

No matter how much I didn't want to eat, I needed to. I needed to drink plenty of water and avoid caffeine. She even gave me a list of food that increases serotonin in the brain. One of the items on this list was pistachios. The paper said to eat a handful twice a day so I tried it. I always liked pistachios, and they really did help. Food still tasted and felt like cardboard, but it only took a little bit to help me feel better.

My therapist also said it was important to go about my day and take my mind off Duane yet it was also important to take time to let the pain out. If I was at work and felt like I was going to cry, she said tell myself that I understand I need to cry but it must wait a little while. At first all of her advice sounded strange, but I tried every suggestion and it really did work. I took advice from everyone. Crysten suggested I listen to 80s music since it was so upbeat and optimistic. She looked thrilled when she came into the office one day and it was playing. The music helped too. Prayer helped me the most. I prayed daily, asking the Lord to give me strength and peace. Each time I prayed, I felt a sense of relief in my heart. Prayer was what helped me the most.

The memorial service at the shelter went well. Not many people showed up. Not because they didn't like Duane, but because they were informed the service was at 3 p.m. However, we had it at 11 a.m. I'm sure some people didn't go because they thought Duane was a jerk, but the people who mattered and knew him well were there. Elijah, Chad, Crysten, Roy, Rosie, a couple other client's, the pastor from Duane's church, along with a young couple Duane had befriended through there as well. The pastor talked about when he first met Duane. It was the summer prior and the church had a festival going on that day.

The shelter took a few of the clients who were interested in going. Duane didn't really want to go but the others talked him into it. The church was doing baptisms that day. Katie was one of the clients who went. She told Duane it may do him some good to get baptized. So he did. The pastor said he could tell Duane was troubled but saw the good in him. He talked Duane into attending the church, which he did but not often. He would go when he felt like he needed help. I remember him telling me that he would look around the room and the church members would look back at him as if they were judging him. It made him feel so uncomfortable to the point he didn't want to attend anymore. I told him it didn't matter what people thought. It only mattered what God thought. He loved Duane and was glad he could make it to church that day.

Some of the stories were happy whereas others were not. Elijah talked about his last conversation with Duane. He said it had lasted awhile, until about 2 am when Elijah had to be at work. If that were the correct time frame, then Duane was still alive when I repeatedly called him. He said Duane called to say he wasn't going to come over as originally planned. Their conversation consisted of Elijah doing most of the talking about this and that. He said there was at least five times where he stopped talking and asked if Duane was still on the line. When Duane wouldn't answer, Elijah would be more persistent, "Are you there? Hello? Hello? Duane?"

"Yep...." Duane mumbled. "I'm still here."

Elijah had mentioned that even though Duane ranted a lot in the past, at least that was the normal Duane. If Duane was bitching about something or someone, it was safe to assume he was ok. Although Duane sounded depressed most of the time, that night on the phone was something else. It was even more serious. Elijah also wishes he would have responded differently that night. He could have saved his friend's life as well.

Rosie talked about when she and Duane would have their weekly meetings. Duane was often irritated about something and she would let him vent to her. Just when she thought he was still upset or worried, she would quickly catch a glimpse of a twinkle in his eye. Then a shy smirk on his face would appear then fade fast when he saw her looking. It was as if he didn't want her or anyone to know that he had happiness inside him that tried to show through occasionally. It made her smile too when she thought about it.

The young couple from church talked about their moments with Duane. They were the ones who let me take a shower when the power went out. They talked about Duane wanting to marry his girlfriend and have children with her. Some of the people knew it was me whereas others were clueless. The couple said that Duane had things to tell me but was afraid I would leave. They told him that since I loved him, I would work out whatever those issues were. A couple of the other clients spoke about goofy moments that they had with Duane while he stayed at the shelter. The pastor said he would gladly answer any questions about the suicide. I told him I was worried that Duane wouldn't go to heaven because he took his own life. I firmly believe that when it's your time to go its God's decision and no one else's.

The pastor said Duane was in God's hands now and that possibly this happened to avoid something else even worse from happening. It is God's decision what happens to him from here. I'd like to believe that Duane went to heaven. Although I disagree with the choice he made, I know he had a good soul and heart and he deserves to be there. I feel in my heart that is where he is. He is there waiting for me. He is waiting for all of us. My soul says he is safe and happy now. He feels the love that he didn't feel here. He is where he belongs. If this was not supposed to happen, it wouldn't have. God let it happen because it was supposed to. God needed Duane to come home and this was the way he was to get there. I just pray that his last thought was a good one. I know he was sad and lonely but I hope he didn't leave here that way.

Chapter 18

Finding Beauty in the Darkness

I had to put this behind me. After the service, I sent Duane's family a copy of the program that Meredith had made. Hilary also sent me a copy of the service she had once she received Duane's ashes. She had a service on the beach. She poured his ashes into the Atlantic Ocean. She said to keep in touch, although it has been almost three years since either one of us sent a letter. They don't know me and I don't know them. The only thing we have in common is we lost someone who we love. I don't want to bother them and bring up the past although I think about them from time to time. I know they think about me too. I'd like to know how they are doing but its best to leave it alone. If they contact me I will gladly answer.

I went through some more of Duane's things. I gave some to Crysten and Roy. Other stuff I tucked away in a memory box. Other belongings I had gotten rid of over the last couple years. Some of it I will cherish forever. Other items just brought too much heartache to keep. From time to time I read Duane's Christmas card that he gave me. The first time I looked at it after his death, it gave me new meaning. At first I thought he was referring to the hepatitis he just found out he may have. Now it meant something completely different. I cried once it dawned on me what he was trying to say. He had planned a while ago to leave here, to leave me. I don't think he wanted to. He wanted to try again. He wanted one last shot at happiness. And when that didn't work out, when his heart was broken again and he couldn't take any more pain, he would end it all. However, suicide doesn't stop the pain. It just gives it to someone else. That someone else was me. The grief I will always feel is the price I pay for loving him. That was what Meredith meant when she said we get hurt in life so we don't forget how to love. Although my heart was ripped into pieces, I wouldn't change anything. I would do it all over again. I would gladly suffer for Duane so he can be eternally happy. I opened up Duane's Christmas card again and reread the sad words:

Denise, my Love.

The Love of my life. I owe you my utmost sincerity. I feel that I owe you my life. I will always and forever treasure the time we've shared. Little or a lot. Whatever the turn out of this trying time in my life, I apologize to you for the terrible decisions I've made that have affected you. You deserve happiness. If I don't make it through I hope you will remember me as a good man. A man of love, honesty, and integrity. If it is my time to go soon, I will not take with me the pain, shame, and regret of life but the love you have allowed me to cherish with you. You are without a doubt in my mind my one and only. I can only hope and pray that God himself, he will allow me to wait for you in heaven. I believe I made peace. I'll be at peace knowing one day you will be there with me. The cruelty of this world has taught me to be strong for at our times of feeding into weakness we will surely pay for. I am paying my final debt. God will forgive us if we ask as long as I forgive those who I swore in the past I never would. I can only hope and pray you forgive me which I can see you already have and always will. You are beautiful inside and out. I should have kept my faith in him that he would give me such a precious gift such as yourself, but I didn't keep my faith. Now I shall suffer for it whereas I very well may have been able to live a loving life with you. I will love you always and forever, death and eternity. I will love you until my final breath and beyond.

Sincerely,

Duane Marcus Cambell Jr.

The letter made me mad too. He was planning on killing himself yet giving me the hope that we would be together for the rest of our lives. If he had chosen to stay that night, what about all the other upcoming nights? I would be in constant worry that he would do this. In my heart I could see him doing it but at the same time I couldn't. Looking back now, he and I never had a chance. We would never be happy. We would want to be together but would never be able to. Our relationship would be the constant vicious unhealthy cycle that we would try and fix yet it could never be fixed. Maybe him gone was the only option. If he were still here, I would want to keep trying. My relationships would suffer. Even if we weren't a couple, I would be worried about him all the time. Was he ok? Did he need anything? I would be jealous of his lovers and I know he would be jealous of mine. We would make up and break up over and over. Yet we wouldn't be able to keep our hands off each other. We would never work it out. But the way we felt about each other would keep us from working out with others. This was the only way to keep us apart and it was better this way, as sad as it sounded.

For a while after Duane passed, my days ran together. I worked all day. Then I would come home late at night and try to sleep the best I could. I did this every day. I had to stay busy. I gave myself time to cry too. I remember one night I was in the bathroom and I was getting ready to take a shower. As I opened up the cupboard to get a towel, I began to cry uncontrollably. The tears were flowing so quickly that I couldn't catch my breath. It felt as though my body was being squeezed. As I paused between sobs to catch a breath, it felt like I was being squeezed even tighter.

Then suddenly I felt as if someone was holding me. It was a very faint feeling, as though someone was barely touching me. I leaned into them like I was resting on a shoulder. I continued to cry on the invisible presence. I felt calmer and safer. It felt like Duane. It was as if he were there to tell me not to cry. *Try not to be sad* his words ran through my mind. He was ok and he wanted me to know that. He wanted me to move on and I could only do that if I knew he was finally happy now. I could also hear him saying he was sorry for what he was putting me and others through. He never wanted to hurt anyone.

That moment I will never forget. To actually feel like someone was holding me was creepy but yet it brought me comfort. After that, I never felt that surreal moment. Yet I never felt so lonely like I did that day. Sometimes I lay awake at night and it hits me that Duane is dead. It has been almost three years but sometimes it dawns on me like it just happened. I feel the panic in my heart that he shot himself and I see disturbing images in my head. That is when I take a sleeping pill to help me calm down and pass out.

The shelter closed in August of 2013. It was a sad moment for me. I was scared about not having a job and losing all I had left. I was worried about where clients were going to go. I realized that memories I had of Duane walking past the office window smiling at me would fade away. At the same time I was relieved. It seemed that after Duane's death I had lost my light there at the housing center. Everywhere I went on grounds, I saw him. Some of our memories made me laugh. Others made me angry. Most of the memories made me sad. I had to go off somewhere secluded to cry for a few minutes before returning to the office. With the shelter closing, a chapter in my life was ending and a new one would begin. Perhaps that was a good thing. Maybe I could finally move on.

Dave and I ended up working things out. We both still loved each other despite all that happened. We realized that we belonged together. Neither one of our lives had felt normal the moment we split. Dave had been okay. He survived without me like I knew he would. But he said he felt emptiness. Every time he entered our home he could feel my presence and see the memories of us. It made his heart ache and he couldn't eat. I suffered immensely, but I know it was my fault. I caused my own pain. Everyone else suffered in some way too. If I hadn't left to be with Duane, I wouldn't be feeling the grief now. I broke our family apart. But the past few months made me realize that my life was great before. I was just too stupid to see it. I appreciated Dave and his family now. The things that bothered me before didn't anymore. They were silly reasons to leave. They were things that could be dealt with. Instead of arguing with Dave about what I hated in our relationship, I could sit down with him now and find solutions. To the things I was blind about before, I could see clearly now. I just couldn't believe it took being with a damaged person and then being completely alone to see it. Although Duane's death has been the most traumatic thing I had to go through, in a way I'm glad I did because it made me a better person.

I think about Duane every day. Some days I think about him more than others. Specific dates stick out so when those days come around again, he is on my brain constantly. January 19th sticks out the most. That was the day the police told me Duane was dead. Even though I knew it in my heart he died right after I saw him two days prior to that, I still focus on the 19th. That day is tough. Not only is it the anniversary of his passing but it is also a very cold and dreary time of year.

I don't do much that day. I go about my business like I would but I am solemn about it. Dave comforts me but gives me my space because he empathizes despite the fact. I do not go anywhere. I do not talk to anyone. My therapist said I should go somewhere private and special on that day. A place that was special to just Duane and I. Since he didn't have a grave, she suggested I have a yearly memorial service alone. Somewhere I can talk to Duane and celebrate his life instead of mourning another year without him. No place like that exists. So I stay at home in sorrow.

I often think about Duane's good and bad points. He had anger issues. He was clinically depressed. He may have even been a little crazy. Those are the things most people will remember. If you ask them about Duane Cambell, those are the words you will hear. For me, Duane was much more. He was *real*. When I say real I don't mean the stories he told. He was a storyteller for sure. I know not everything he told me and others were true. When I say real, I mean he didn't sugar coat how he felt about people. He told you like it was, no matter how crazy it sounded. He cared about people even though he played it off like he didn't. He didn't want to hurt people. When he realized his actions did hurt someone, he tried his hardest to make it right. He had a huge heart. He always helped others even when he didn't have much to give. He even helped out people who were unkind in return.

There was a time he told me about his stay at the shelter. There was going to be thorough room inspections because clients were dropping dirty on their drug tests. He held onto drugs for his roommate so the guy wouldn't get caught with them. The person he was helping was someone who made a false police report about him a short time before. Although it pissed Duane off, he didn't want this person to get kicked out and possibly lose everything they had gained from being there. He let what happened before go so he could do the right thing now. That was what Duane did. Duane was so real. He was one of the realest people I had ever met. He was true.

I try to think about the happy times with Duane and not so much of the end. I want to remember him in a positive way. I don't want to think about his final moments and how he chose to leave this world. I try to think about the parts of Duane that I loved and not the things I hated. Although Duane was often angry or in despair, there were plenty of good times. I remember one night we were at my house listening to music. The song *"Down in a hole"* by Alice in Chains came on. It was a slower rock song. I asked Duane to slow dance with me. He admitted he never danced with anyone before.

"You never went to a school dance?" I asked in shock.

"Never," Duane shook his head shyly. I was in disbelief. I couldn't believe he had never gone to a school dance. I thought surely every child got to experience that.

"I'll show you." I said taking his hand. I put his arms around my waist then I placed my arms around his neck.

"Just slowly turn with the music," I explained, resting my head on his shoulder. "Just feel the beat."

Within a few seconds, Duane was in rhythm with me as we slowly swayed and turned our bodies right with the rhythm of the song. He was a quick learner. The dance was perfect. Our bodies leaned in closer and I felt like we had melted into one. It was so comfortable in his arms. I didn't want this moment to end. Before we realized, the song had ended and the next one began to play. It wasn't until that song was halfway over before we realized that.

"I liked that," Duane smiled. "That was nice."

He wanted to dance some more. We continued to hold each other and swayed to the upcoming slower beats. While we held each other, we talked about how each song we heard could possibly be our wedding song. We talked about having a gothic themed wedding and I would wear a red dress instead of white. My bouquet would be black roses. The tables would be decorated with black and red butterflies. It was a conversation we would have many times. He seemed to like the idea of marriage. He just wanted to belong to somebody and have a place he could actually refer to as home.

I think about the silly moments where he would take a song and change the words. It would make me laugh hysterically. I think about the tickling and Duane chasing me around the house. I loved his playful side. I think about the long talks over coffee where he confided in me his darkest and most intimate details growing up. I think about the full body massages he would give me after a stressful day at work. I missed all of that.

Despite all the negative things about him, just being real and true canceled out all of them. I fortunately got to know him like most didn't. He went from being the scariest person to the most loving. Even if we hadn't developed a sexual and romantic relationship, I know in my heart Duane would make a great friend. He was a friend who would be there and who wouldn't judge. Duane definitely fits the saying *"Don't judge a book by its cover."* He truly was one of the best.

www.ingramcontent.com/pod-product-compliance
Lightning Source LLC
Chambersburg PA
CBHW072004060426
42446CB00042B/1827